FLESH FOR FANTASY

FLESH FOR FANTASY

Producing and Consuming Exotic Dance

R. Danielle Egan, Katherine Frank, & Merri Lisa Johnson

THUNDER'S MOUTH PRESS
NEW YORK

FLESH FOR FANTASY

Producing and Consuming Exotic Dance

Published by
Thunder's Mouth Press
An Imprint of Avalon Publishing Group Inc.
245 West 17th Street, 11th Floor
New York, NY 10011

First printing January 2006

Library of Congress Cataloging-in-Publication Data is available.

ISBN: 1-56025-721-0
ISBN 13: 978-1-56025-721-9

9 8 7 6 5 4 3 2 1

Book design by Maria E. Torres
Printed in the United States of America
Distributed by Publishers Group West

In Memory of
Shelly Manaster

Contents

SECTION THREE: Reformulations

Acknowledgments

This volume has been a long time in production and has seen a variety of forms; because of this it would be impossible to thank all of the individuals who somehow lent their influence to this work. It has indeed been a collaborative project from its very beginnings. Ex-stripper and activist Kelly Holsopple originally approached Katherine Frank with the idea for a volume on stripping entirely written by strippers. Although Kelly decided to leave the project to pursue a different career path, her commitment to the idea of women involved in stripping being the ones to ask the questions and set the terms of the debates around the industry is one that we have strived to uphold. Over the years, pieces were added and cut, revised and reworked, and we would like to thank the contributors for their patience, hard work, and creativity at each phase.

We would like to thank the individuals who helped with the production logistics. Mary Haught provided invaluable help with the paperwork and the preparation of the manuscript. There are also people who have provided support for each of us in a multitude of other ways—commenting on pieces, allowing us the time to write and strategize, or simply being there when we needed them. Finally, Thunder's Mouth Press has been enjoyable to work with, and we would like to thank the individuals there who have helped with this manuscript at each stage of its production.

Introduction

Third Wave Strippers: Flesh for Feminist Fantasy

R. Danielle Egan, Katherine Frank, and Merri Lisa Johnson

We thought we were the only ones.

Finding each other as colleagues and coeditors startled us with bolts of pleasure and recognition, though the creation of our threesome looked initially like a moment of Las Vegas luck, three sequined figures lining up against statistical probabilities. It turns out the odds were in our favor all along. As we have come to realize, we are part of a generation of women currently entering the workforce as professors, researchers, lawyers, and other professionals who also worked during some part of our lives in the sex industry. We came of age as professionals in the era of riot grrl and gender trouble, navigating the backlash of postfeminism and the subversions of poststructuralism. Picture us: cadres of college-age feminists picking up our notebooks and our copies of feminist philosopher Judith Butler's *Bodies that Matter* after a scintillating, or perhaps unsatisfying, women's studies class, getting in our cars, and driving across town to the local strip club to work out our own personal understandings of gender performativity, parodic subversion, and the high drag of the third wave feminist stripper.

Poststructuralism, for all its popularity as a theory that provides insight into the fragmentation of identities in a postmodern era while radically calling into question the master narratives of our culture, has been accused of being excessively abstract in its treatment of gender and sexuality. Moved by poststructuralism's insights, but frustrated by its lack of materiality, our editorial collective of third wave strippers wants to see, precisely, *whose* bodies matter, *how* bodies matter, and to whom. So we open our lockers, pull out leather whips or feather boas, racy schoolgirl costumes or floor-length white dresses that shimmer under the lights, and we ascend the stage, or hover our hips over a young man's lap, or grind against his zipper with a thin thread of spandex as our barely there barrier. We sip champagne in the fantasy rooms or VIP suites with businessmen and blind men, single men and married men, men with wandering hands but nothing to say and men who pay us to sit and chat without ever asking to see us naked. We count our money at the end of the night, awash in sweat and glitter, side by side with college students, single moms, professional women looking to augment their incomes, young girls anxious to rebel, and women who just don't know what else to do. We pack up our schoolbooks and stripper gear—coinciding sources of poststructuralist theory on this question of bodies that matter—and we try to find out.

As women who have shifted positions within and between strip clubs, classrooms, courtrooms, and boardrooms, flexing our feet in Lucite stilettos and sensible flats, adorning ourselves in velvet gowns and elbow-length gloves by night, confining ourselves in button-down blouses and pencil skirts by day, we have inhabited the socially sanctioned forms of femininity as well as its margins. An amalgamation of many femininities, we embody the multiple subject positions critical scholars theorize in discussions of postmodern identity and intersectional analysis: good girls and bad girls, virgins and whores, and acceptable bodies and their transgressive counterparts. We offer in this collection of essays our version of "lived theory" or "theory in the flesh," borrowing these terms from bell hooks, Gloria Anzaldua, and Cherrie Moraga, who mounted a critique of hegemonic second wave feminism from the perspectives of women of color. In *Flesh for Fantasy,* we infuse the notion of "theory in the flesh" with another marginalized perspective in feminism—that of the sex worker—asking once again how feminist theories of power, sexuality, and the body might change if they were more substantially informed by the embodied knowledge of sex workers and patrons of the sex industry.

In strip clubs, onstage and at the customers' tables, our dancer bodies take on a fantasy hue. The black lights, the costumes, the makeup, the height of the stages, the music, the movement, and the customers' expectations all interact with each other to perfect our flaws. What you see on the stage is not what you see behind the scenes, in the dressing rooms of the club, or in our bedrooms at home. This same mix of lighting and setting can also highlight our vulnerabilities, exposing our fears in the form of what a customer sees when he does not find a dancer attractive and what we see if we suddenly turn self-conscious or otherwise fall short of a successful performance. Some observers of exotic dance see the stripper as a powerful female figure on her rightful pedestal; others see a woman who is confused and degraded. Some observers view our bodies and see disease, immorality, and plummeting property values. Other observers project shame, guilt, jealousy, or sexual desire onto our flesh. Imagine that we can freeze a moment in time at a strip club. Look at the woman twirling onstage, hands unhooking her breakaway thong. Or behind her, at the dancer on the couch, flipping her hair against a customer's torso. Whose fantasy is this? Our answer follows no easy formula.

Like many third wave feminist anthologies, *Flesh for Fantasy* foregrounds ambivalence as a key characteristic of our position on sex work and complexity as the root of our experiences.[1] While we cannot claim that every contributor to this volume explicitly identifies as a feminist, or even believes that feminism is the most promising way to analyze or create changes in the sex industry or in society more generally, the three of us *do* identify as feminists, and when we were selecting pieces for this volume we chose those pieces that spoke to us and to the issues that concerned us about sex work. Our stories about stripping, along with the stories of the other contributors, embody contradictions between the competing cultural narratives of feminism and entrenched gender inequalities, materialist critique and late capitalist consumption, and sexual libertarianism and sexual prescriptivism. Our voices crack. We hold parts of all these cultural influences in our bodies, in our desires, in our politics, and we are not always sure how we feel about this mixture at a particular given time. There is a longing within us to pronounce to the world that as a post-civil rights generation—a generation of girl power and *Girls Gone Wild*—we can do whatever we want, including taking our clothes off for money. This longing stems from a utopian wish for a world that was freer of bias, stigma, and violence than the one we actually live in. Yet since we put our theories into practice in an intensely embodied way, our nude bodies on display, we are brought back to certain painful realities about sexism and sex worker stigma on a regular basis. This collection holds both of these impulses together—the utopian desire to declare the world safe for strippers and the realist corrective of reminding ourselves and our readers that stripping often hurts us, physically and psychologically—without subordinating one to the other. As third wave feminist dancers, we acknowledge the paradoxes of simultaneously being subject to and subversive toward existing systems of power.

The efforts among third wave feminists to destigmatize sex work are often perceived as antagonistic to the goals of second wave feminism. However, the self-reflexive writings of third wave feminist strippers do not necessarily oppose second wave feminism; rather, they pick up on the sex positive and sex radical positions within the second wave that have too often been obscured by mainstream media and movement spokespersons. Writer and activist Pat Califia argues that "being a sex radical means being defiant as well as deviant. It means being aware that there is something unsatisfying and dishonest about the way sex is talked about (or hidden) in daily life. It also means questioning the way our society assigns privilege based on adherence to its moral codes, and in fact makes every sexual choice a matter of morality. If you believe that these inequalities can be addressed only through extreme social change, then you qualify as a sex radical, even if you prefer to get off in the missionary position and still believe there are only two genders."[2]

A sex radical third wave feminist position recognizes that sex and sex work can "destabilize male power as well as reinforce it."[3] There is no preordained meaning to sex work—it is neither inherently feminist nor inherently oppressive. Rather, it is carried out under certain political, economic, and ideological conditions that must be explored, challenged, and revisioned. In recent years, several books, such as *Whores and Other Feminists, Live Sex Acts, Real Live Nude Girl,* and *Global Sex Workers,* have made important interventions in this area for both academic and more general audiences. This collection continues these investigations, although we narrow our focus to stripping and rely primarily on autoethnographic writing from individuals who have been intimately involved with the work. Our approach in this text takes seriously the strategies outlined by feminist writer Lynn Chancer in her effort to reconcile key differences within feminism:

> [I]n order to become a movement genuinely concerned about the lives of *all* women, any satisfactory third wave would have to view a question supposedly "sexual" like reproductive rights and a supposedly "economic" issue like women's ongoing impoverishment with equal political seriousness and alarm. *Both* problems—the realizing of sexual *and* economic freedoms so that genuine choices are possible in both arenas—should be occasioning huge demonstrations and protests led by large numbers of feminists committed to bettering all women's lives.[4]

We couldn't agree more, and our exploration of exotic dance borrows Chancer's vision of combining the supposedly sexual issue of dancing nude with the clearly economic issue of dancers being asked to sell promotional T-shirts to their customers along with table dances and being required to cover the cost of the shirts if they don't make the sale, to name just one of the ways management dips into the garters of its hardworking entertainers. Susan Bremer's piece, along with others in this volume, explores the nuances of club policies and their impacts on dancers; Magdalene Meretrix examines the effects of local regulations—which often involve an underlying economic motive—on the women attempting to negotiate them successfully.

Although the essays in this collection often focus explicitly on stripping, many of the contributors have engaged in different forms of sex work over the years. In some cases, the editors and contributors address "sex work" or the "sex industry" more generally, including pornography, prostitution, professional domination, massage parlors, strip clubs, and peep shows in our analyses. Other times, the unique aspects of stripping take center stage. Analytic specificity is important in critiques of the sex industry—stripping requires a different kind of labor and occupies a different legal zone than prostitution, for example—but it is equally important to examine the commercialization of sexual services as a whole. In this way, alliances among a wide range of sex workers become possible without erasing the particular shape of the exotic dancer's struggle for improved labor conditions, as well as variations *among* exotic dancers in different regions and types of clubs.

Given our positions as former strippers and as academic feminists, we take certain elements of the sex industry as axiomatic in our writing, especially the existence of a sometimes maddening complexity to the work. We do not want to ignore or downplay the pleasurable, exciting, or transgressive aspects of stripping that some women experience, nor the practical financial rewards. On the other hand, because we've all experienced firsthand some of the more negative aspects of the industry, we do not feel the need to uncritically defend exotic dance as it now exists. We've been there and might want to return. We certainly do not want to prevent anyone else from working in or visiting the clubs, or from agitating to make things better for those who make their living or spend their leisure time inside.

With this volume, we hope to challenge certain practices within the sex industry without advocating abolition, draconian regulation, or simple condemnation of the practices and desires expressed in either the production or consumption of sexualized services. We want to move the discourse on exotic dance beyond debates about whether dancers feel exploited or exercise agency, questions repeatedly asked in both academic and popular forums, to a focus on concrete explorations of particular workplace experiences and policies, legal regulations, or customer behaviors that cause working conditions in the clubs to improve or deteriorate. We take for granted that no one actor or group in the strip club wields complete power over the others involved. Rather, power is exchanged and negotiated among the customers, dancers, managers, club owners, and legal enforcers. Yet we also want to explore the cultural discourses, beliefs, and practices that cause dancers in different parts of the country and different clubs to experience some of the same pleasures, as well as similar frustrations and limitations.

STRIPPING IN THE U.S.A.

Like any other cultural phenomenon, exotic dance changes over time. In the days of burlesque, and especially in the 1920s and 1930s, striptease was a highly controversial practice, though the emphasis fell more heavily on "tease" than "strip," since dancers mainly performed short, titillating dance numbers with little to no actual nudity. In its contemporary format, striptease can be usefully situated within a broad gendered service industry—ranging from flight attendants to Hooters girls to strippers—in which women provide both erotic fantasy and emotional support to customers in addition to their visual displays and performances.[5]

Although stripping can be housed within a larger rubric of sexualized services (along with prostitution, pornography, massage parlors, and lingerie shows), its position as simultaneously deviant and legal separates it from other forms of erotic labor. It is an ambiguously permitted cultural practice, functioning as a cornerstone of masculine leisure and rites of passage, yet bearing stigma for certain customers (the regulars) as well as for most dancers. Stripping is also uniquely interactive, with "real live nude girls" available for viewing within very specific limits (sometimes a glass pane separates the customer from the dancer; sometimes a club rule of anywhere from six inches to two feet; sometimes, in the case of lapdancing, only the thin cotton fabric of a customer's sweatpants comes between him and the object of his fantasy). As Holly Bell, Lacey Sloan, and Chris Strickling argue, strippers "sell an *image* of female sexuality, as do those who engage in print pornography," but at the same time, strippers "are present at the moment of consumption." There is thus "a level of immediacy in this exchange that goes beyond the kind of representation of female sexuality encountered in pornography" and makes the work distinctive.[6] The interactive nature of striptease also challenges us to think more precisely about what the customers are purchasing in their transactions, as Egan and Frank's contributions to this collection explore.

Transitions within the sex industry in general, and strip clubs in particular, emerge in response to dynamic interchanges between capital (the shift from modern to postmodern forms of labor), new forms of technology (VCR, DVDs, and the Internet), and changing discourses on sexuality and gender post-sexual revolution. Striptease, like the rest of the adult-entertainment industry, grew rapidly over the past several decades. In 1998, there were over three thousand strip clubs in the United States; with this increase we have also seen the emergence of exotic dance franchises and clubs being traded on the NASDAQ exchange.[7] A commonly noted feature of late capitalism is that more and more forms of entertainment become preoccupied with the commodification of spectacle and experience. Certainly the proliferation of strip clubs can be offered as an example of the profitability of this strategy. Indeed it makes perfect sense that strip clubs should multiply so wildly in the United States during the last several decades, along with the panic about AIDS and fears about the dissolution of "the family." The process of upscaling in strip clubs, with its promise of clean and respectable interactions, could alleviate certain fears about contamination and disease that escalated around prostitution. The fact that sexual activity is not generally expected or offered in strip clubs also fits well with a growing emphasis on monogamy and marriage for heterosexuals after the sexual experimentation (and ensuing disillusionment for many) of the 1970s. Numerous other social changes may also be influencing this rapid increase in strip clubs in the United States: the increased presence of women in the workforce, a continued backlash against feminism and the idea of "political correctness," ongoing and concerted marketing efforts to sexualize and masculinize particular forms of consumption ("sports, beer, and women," for example), changing patterns of mobility that have influenced dating practices and the formation of intimate partnerships, and changes in the nature of work that involve more out-of-town travel for businessmen and thus more anonymous opportunities to purchase commodified sexualized services, to name just a few.[8]

There are many different kinds of strip clubs, ranging from small neighborhood pubs or bars clustered together in warehouse zones or red-light districts to upscale "gentlemen's clubs," which are sometimes multimillion-dollar entertainment complexes. Depending on the geographic location and the local laws and regulations, strip clubs also offer different kinds of services to their clients—ranging from full-contact lap dances (which may sometimes result in sexual release for the customer) to hands-off table dancing and with varying amounts of nudity (bikinis, nipple pasties, topless, bottomless). Some clubs serve bar food; others offer fine dining. Some allow alcoholic beverages on the premises; others serve only beer and wine or soft drinks. One might find four or more stages in constant operation and dozens of glamorously dressed dancers circulating about the room, three or four women rotating sets on a single stage, or a collection of dancers behind the glass of a peep show.

Changes in the services offered inside the clubs also shift with social and economic changes, technological innovations, and the legal climate. The introduction of the VCR and cable television in the 1980s and the Internet in the 1990s shifted pornography from shadowy theaters in bad neighborhoods to the privacy and comfort of one's own home. Leading the video industry in home sales, pornography boomed and strip-club attendance began to slump.[9] In response, exotic dance clubs offered more specialized and creative spectacles and services such as topless or nude female wrestling and, in certain states, increased physical contact between dancers and customers. Clubs compete with each other through advertising and marketing strategies, the appearances and comportment of their dancers, food and beverage specials, the installation of private VIP rooms and conference areas, special performances by traveling feature dancers, the provision of additional services inside the clubs, including massages, opportunities for extended interaction with particular dancers, bathroom attendants, liquor models, and broadcasting pay-per-view sports events.

Exotic dance is, according to anthropologist and dance scholar Judith Hanna, "a lightning rod" for cultural conflict over bodily display and over when, where, and for whom such display constitutes an acceptable form of sexual expression. The opposition to strip clubs and other forms of sex work is often quite well organized. Groups such as the National Family Legal Foundation draw on discourses of public and private morality to bolster their attacks against such establishments.[10] The U.S. Supreme Court has taken up questions about the regulation of exotic dance in Barnes vs. Glenn Theater, Inc., in 1991, and again in 2000 with Erie vs. Pap's A.M. In both of these cases, the Supreme Court justices ruled to give states greater rights in controlling the practices in exotic dance clubs and creating laws that would make it significantly harder to operate such establishments.[11] Though exotic dance is given minimal protections as a form of expressive conduct, there has been a tendency in both the upper and lower courts to allow local municipalities to enact restrictive zoning regulations based on claims that strip clubs lead to adverse "secondary effects" in surrounding areas. Zoning laws instated in New York City in 1995, for example, forced many sexually oriented establishments to relocate or substantially adapt their operations. Similar zoning laws and ordinances have been instituted in cities around the nation, resulting in sometimes humorous attempts by strip clubs and their employees to circumvent the restrictions on bodily display or comportment. An ordinance passed in 2001 in Boise, Idaho, for example, banned public nudity except in instances where it had "serious artistic merit"; clearly an attempt to crack down on bodily display in strip clubs without also censoring art classes, plays, or other kinds of performances. With a spark of creativity that must be maddening to the City Council who supported the ordinance, a local strip club now allows dancers to forgo their G-strings and pasties on "Art Club Nights," where customers purchase art materials and try their hands at figure sketching.[12] At the same time, the widespread corporatization of strip clubs means that dancers are subject to increasing restrictions on their workplace autonomy by the clubs themselves, the implementation of higher stage fees, large tip-outs to other club employees, excessive fines, and the same kinds of "speed-ups" as employees in other businesses endure (mandatory two-for-one dance specials, obligatory merchandise sales). Dancers have begun asking for the implementation of standard labor practices in the clubs, as well as a means to hold club owners accountable to those standards.[13] At the same time, activists and strippers frequently disagree about what exactly needs to be changed, what would constitute "improvement" in a workplace, and how to go about organizing and prioritizing their resistances. Not only does a moralizing concern around "family values" grate against one of free sexual expression, but differing beliefs about the roots of sexism, the quest for gender equality, the effects of capitalism and its spread to forms of intimate life, and the neutrality or potential harm of popular forms of entertainment add fuel to the fires.

Almost any crackdown on exotic dance clubs will hit the dancers hardest. Stuck between the expectations of customers, financial imperatives, the look-the-other-way coercions of management, and the long arm of the law, dancers must choreograph some truly intricate footwork to negotiate the ever-changing regulations, and they don't always succeed. To wit: twenty-four strippers were arrested in Myrtle Beach, South Carolina, on August 17, 2004, for violating a county ordinance that requires dancers to wear pasties. These women were hauled off to jail in the middle of a shift because their pasties were not "opaque enough and large enough to hide what they are supposed to cover," according to the *Sun News*. The newspaper's silly circumlocution aside (why use the euphemistic phrase "what they are supposed to cover" instead of just using the word "nipples"?), one might ask who was genuinely at fault here? Without any inside information on the case, we can only surmise that the managers of the clubs permitted and approved these faulty pasties, or at the very least, turned their heads so as not to impede the financial imperatives of their employees. Beyond the managers, one might look to the ordinance itself for the root of the problem. The 1999 South Carolina Supreme Court case, Restaurant Row Associates and The Afterdeck, Inc. d/b/a Thee DollHouse, Petitioners vs. Horry County, lays out the issue as one of zoning. According to current zoning laws in Horry County, adult entertainment establishments cannot be located within five hundred feet of a residential district. In order to modify their business to fit this rule, Thee DollHouse instituted the requirement of pasties and billed itself as an "Adult Cabaret." The pasties used at Thee DollHouse are flesh-colored bits of latex, daubed on the nipples in a liquid form that hardens with air and must be removed with a chemical solvent that can damage the nipples after repeated use. When you look at the dancers onstage, it is not immediately apparent that they are wearing pasties. These are not the sequined, tassled, leopard-print pasties of the burlesque era. They are a creative response to a loophole in the law, and in their insubstantiality, they point to the emptiness of the ordinance, revealing that it too is just for show, a gesture to appease local developers, homeowners, and non-adult business owners. In that these pasties do not have a substantial impact on the type of exotic entertainment available and therefore do not really affect customers, managers, or owners, their main effect is to create another hoop for dancers to jump through, one more piece of equipment to buy for work, one more way to overstep the boundaries of the law and, possibly, end up with a police record.

As strip clubs have increasingly come under fire in communities across the nation in recent years, questions about the nature of exotic dance have taken on a dire importance for women working in the industry. Regulations against certain kinds of contact between dancers and customers can sometimes make stripping safer and more comfortable for dancers, while at other times regulations can be used to drive clubs out of business, prohibiting women from interacting with each other and with the customers in ways that they enjoy, and otherwise harassing employees. Given the opposition to the very existence of strip clubs in many locales, fighting simply to stay in business may take precedence among exotic dancers over more specific battles for labor rights or critiques of gender inequality. When complaints about unfair workplace policies or unsafe work environments may be used as fodder by those wanting the clubs eradicated, giving voice to this dissatisfaction can create counterproductive results. Women working as strippers frequently find themselves in the difficult position of vigorously defending their work in some circles against claims that it is immoral, degrading, or a form of social vice, and simultaneously attempting to critique and challenge exploitative, unsafe, or uncomfortable workplace conditions in other settings.

The variations between strip clubs in terms of services offered, local regulations, and contextual factors, of course, lead to a diversity of workplace experiences, interpretations, and recommendations. Further, as several of the following essays make clear, women's workplace experiences may change from year to year, shift to shift, set to set, or even customer to customer. Dancers' occupational strategies may include going to elaborate lengths to choreograph a stage show or simply performing the same basic routines to every song and collecting their tips with a scowl or smile. Some women choose stripping as one of many different employment options; some choose it in response to limited opportunities to support themselves doing other kinds of work. Their family and educational backgrounds, daily lives and relationships, and future goals and possibilities are as diverse as those of any other population brought together in a workplace, perhaps more so because of the usually temporary nature of the job. One can't dance forever, after all, thus it is always a stepping stone on the way to some other form of work. Some women will look back on stripping as one of the best jobs they ever had, while others may despise those years. The experiences of women in stripping, like those of employees in other industries, are influenced by inequalities of social class, racism, sexism, and homophobia. It is impossible, or at least counterproductive, to ignore the complexity and diversity of women's experiences in this branch of the sex industry. Ultimately, however, we believe that women working *in* stripping should be influential in formulating the questions asked *about* stripping (it is probably safe to say that most of us who work as dancers would rather not encounter another academic researcher or reporter asking if we've been sexually abused, hate all men, or are exhibitionists in the clinical sense) and in searching for solutions to the problems that *do* exist.

Sexuality is beset by contradictions, and, as is recognized in feminist and social theory, often operates as a site of social control. American culture is characterized by rigid sexual boundaries and widespread sexual spectacles (found in advertising, sex manuals, popular music lyrics, music videos, talk shows, films, and a booming sex industry). Our cultural imagination is thus simultaneously hypersexual (wanting sex, selling sex, and making sex a spectacle) and sexually repressive for certain groups of people (claiming that sex is sacred, private, and something to be shared only within monogamous heterosexual relations). Stripper's bodies bear the marks of a cultural preoccupation with sexual boundary setting and transgression, with consequences ranging from familial outrage to collegial titillation, legal difficulties to child custody battles. Many dancers still face a good deal of stigma for their choices and are subject to forms of harassment, misunderstanding, and even violence.

Yet marginalization has its privileges as well as its disadvantages. As adult-film actor Ira Levine points out, "one real advantage" of sex work can be "the freedom of being a leper. After you've already done something loathsome to the majority of the population, you have a certain amount of latitude."[14] Transgressing the boundaries of respectable female virtue, for example, offers certain freedoms from the dizzying rules many of us were taught as young girls: be sexual but not too sexual, be interested but not too interested, enjoy sex but only with one person. Losing your reputation can provide you with "a latitude of speculation" otherwise unavailable to women, to borrow a phrase from *The Scarlet Letter*. Or, as Leora Tanenbaum writes in *Slut!: Growing Up with a Bad Reputation,* being labeled a slut can reveal the goal of good womanhood as a farce.[15] Sex work can lead to a different perspective on how a woman could, or should, relate to her sexuality, as Frank explores in one of her pieces here, "Keeping Her Off the Pole."

The male customers also face stigma and misunderstanding about their desires to visit strip clubs. Dominant cultural beliefs about male sexuality accept and almost dictate that "boys will be boys," leading many men to find themselves held near-hostage in the overdetermined rites of passage for the American male—bachelor parties and birthday parties—which involve tipping a dancer for her time onstage or on their laps. In marked contrast, men who come to clubs by themselves to spend time and money fall outside the parameters of acceptable sexual behavior. Viewed as deviant and untrustworthy, male regulars often face chastising remarks from friends and family for their "perverse" pleasures. The male contributors to our collection highlight the paradoxes of masculine privilege and the cultural stigma attached to those who get labeled as sick, desperate, perverts, or misogynists. Particularly striking is the fact that several of the male contributors to this volume have used pseudonyms to avoid this kind of censure in their everyday lives. The customers' pieces take up the complex emotional aspects of their visits, a strange brew of pleasure and discomfort, desire and guilt, moments of recognized privilege, and feelings of powerlessness. We hope their writings bolster more dialogue on the complex interests that men have in the sex industry—physical, emotional, and economic.

Stripping has certainly become somewhat more respectable in recent years, at least in some circles and when compared with other forms of sex work, and as Alison Fensterstock notes in one of her pieces for this volume, "stripper chic" is being marketed and sold at ever increasing rates. Some girls find a certain cachet in their work as exotic dancers and do not feel the need to hide their employment from friends or family and there are more and more role models for young women (and men) wishing to make a career in the sex industry. Exotic dance has been showcased on television talk shows (*Jenny Jones, Ricki Lake, Jerry Springer*), in soft-core cable documentaries (*G-string Divas, Real Sex*), and at the prestigious Sundance Film Festival (*Live Nude Girls Unite*). Popular representations of stripping continue to multiply—in feature films (*Closer, Exotica, Showgirls, Striptease*), indie films (*The Center of the World, Dancing at the Blue Iguana*), B movies (*Stripped to Kill* and the whole genre of stripper-revenge films), cable television dramas (*The Sopranos, Carnivale*), exercise and self-esteem building videos (*The S Factor: Strip Workouts for Every Woman, The Art of Sensual Dance for Every Body*), books on how to strip for your lover at home (*Bedroom Games*) or how to get a job at a strip club (*Nice Job*), beautiful photographic essays (*Lap-dancer*), and a spate of stripper memoirs (*Ivy League Stripper, Strip City, Bare: On Women, Dancing, Sex and Power, Stripper Shoes, Diary of a Stripper,* and *Confessions of a Stripper: Tales from the VIP Room*). In her piece for this volume, Merri Lisa Johnson explores some of the complexities of these various media representations. Clearly, exotic dance has the American public hot and bothered—eyes open, wallets out.

SEX RADICAL AUTOETHNOGRAPHY

The use of "flesh for fantasy" as the title of this collection is about the many ways that dancers' bodies become the material of fantasy for different groups of people—in strip clubs, in media representations, in the law. The flesh of strippers—our own flesh and the flesh of the women we enjoy watching—can be material for our own fantasies, as feminists, of a sex-positive erotic revolution. It can be part of the dark underbelly of our sexuality, the place where we try to come to terms with the powerful emotions of desire, shame, love, and anger through fantasies of power, control, or submission. The fact that we are also flesh for men's fantasies, or that our bodies become the premise on which antiporn feminists argue the inherent sexism of the sex industry or on which conservative groups argue against moral and physical decay, is neither wholly unproblematic for us, nor is it the determining power dynamic. As the title song, Billy Idol's "Flesh for Fantasy," asks, "Ain't it strange what we do to feel alright?" All three editors of this collection have, at some point, danced nude to this song, a strip-club classic. The meanings we created in our own minds as we reveled in the irreverence of our own spectacle often differed substantially from the meanings created in the customers' minds or in the mainstream cultural perception of the stripper as victim or object. Indulging in the pleasure of our own nakedness and in the active motions of our minds as we fantasize a new version of ourselves, arching and spinning and grinning through our open legs, this is our "sex attack," our "change in pace." At times, of course, our sex radical attacks on the ideologies that confine us and threaten to define us are thwarted by recalcitrant flesh; our fantasies are co-opted by our audiences, our managers, our co-workers, local interest groups, or even by parts of ourselves. Nothing is ever guaranteed, as Shelly Manaster's melancholy contributions to this collection so powerfully illustrate. By lifting the standard strip-club music fare of Billy Idol's song for our title, we reproduce the parodic recontextualizations that we performed in the strip clubs, taking our scholarly bodies and employing them with lap dances, balancing our efforts to negotiate social expectations and norms of gendered behavior, customer preferences, and our own private fantasies and significances.

As white middle-class women who have the time, financial security, and institutional or personal support to undertake this project of theorizing exotic dance, we recognize that we cannot speak for all dancers and we do not claim to do so. All three of the editors worked as strippers out of choice rather than necessity, and we knew we could quit at any time—a position of privilege that differs starkly from many women whose options are more limited due to race, class, and education. We enjoyed mobility within the sex industry and between different strata of strip clubs, as well as a choice of which kinds of erotic labor we preferred. Our cultural and educational capital was often (though not always) an asset in interactions with the customers and management of the clubs. Most of the other contributors to this text share our race and current class privilege and most have postgraduate education; as such, the text is necessarily limited in its representation of racial and economic diversity of experience. There were, in fact, a number of women who were asked to contribute who were not able to do so because of the demands of sex work, motherhood, academic life, or career. However, we hope the writings here spark dialogue, engaging more participants in an ongoing conversation over time.

Second wave feminist consciousness-raising groups showed women that their personal lives, far from being inconsequential, could be catalysts for political organizing. What once seemed like private and personal discontents and difficulties (from house cleaning to domestic violence) shifted to being viewed as sites of political engagement and collective action, and this resulted in the formation of new political discourses and transformative imagery. Speaking out constituted a first step for women toward imagining their lives and the world as different in the future, as extricated, even somewhat, from sexist social structures. The movement for rights among the gay, lesbian, bisexual, transgender, and queer or questioning community also experienced this momentous shift from the isolation of the closet to the liberation of group identity and voice, or, in gay historian Jonathan Ned Katz's words, "from a sense of ourselves as individual monster-freaks to a new, shared sense of ourselves as outraged resisters."[16] With similar ends in mind, we employ autoethnography as a sex radical attempt to render our personal experiences political. Autoethnographic writing, a hybrid genre of growing popularity in cultural anthropology and in other disciplines, places individual experience in broader sociohistorical contexts. Each essay here interweaves thick description and critical analysis of differing levels, teasing new meaning from the taken-for-granted aspects of striptease. Far beyond the desire to confess our transgressions or capitalize on stripping's sensationalistic cachet, *Flesh for Fantasy* is devoted to destigmatizing the sex industry, illuminating the labor conditions of strippers, and revising the cultural connotations of exotic dance.

We hope ultimately to encourage new conceptualizations of what strip clubs could and should be: what would the sex industry look like in a more sex-positive society? Califia notes that the sex industry is shaped by several negative forces in contemporary America: because the work is often illegal or on the borderline of acceptability, it may "attract people who are desperate, who believe they have few or no other choices, and people who embrace the identities of rebel, outsider, and criminal," that is, the stigma and illegality may mean that people who would actually enjoy sex work may choose other paths. Furthermore, it caters to those who would compartmentalize female sexuality, and it may overlap with other underground economies. Finally, it may offer one of the only forms of employment for unskilled laborers.[17] Yet Califia also poses the hypothetical question of what the industry could look like if some of these forces and constraints were lifted. Unlike social critics who predict that commercial sex would whither away in the face of gender equality or the eradication of capitalism, Califia argues that perhaps there would always be those people who would want to buy and sell sexual services. Some individuals, for example, might always want to partake in the sex industry, either because they are too busy to find partners, demand specialized services, want sex without commitment, or want the thrill of new partners they might not be able to woo without financial remuneration. There may also always be those who desire to work in the sex industry, and social change might alter possibilities so that only individuals who desire to work in the sex industry do so.

At the very least, we can begin to work toward a situation where strip clubs and other sex-industry venues can become safe and sexy places that treat their workers fairly and their customers well.

We are not individual freaks.

We are part of a community that resists the compartmentalization of sexuality from the rest of our lives and desires to challenge the hypocrisy that surrounds commercialized sexuality. We are working toward a shared sense of ourselves as advocates of gender justice, sexual freedom, safe work environments, and the importance of erotic play.

And we are not the only ones.

SECTION ONE: Friction

1

Treading Water: An Autoethnographic Account(ing) of the Lap Dance

Shelly Manaster

Treading water is a way of pausing, conserving energy, and taking a moment for the purpose of remaining stationary in an environment that ultimately demands movement on your part, if only because it has the potential to consume your energy before you can reach safety. After treading there are really only three choices: to swim forward, to swim back, or to drown.

APPROACHING RECOGNITION

One year ago in San Francisco I saw a girl walking across the street while I was stopped in a car waiting for the light to change. It was somewhere between Van Ness and O'Farrell and Market and Fifth, in those blocks behind the strip clubs that girls would venture into drunk to pick up a bottle before work. She was midway through the crosswalk when she stopped—I had noticed her before on the streets, but had not seen her face. She was wearing a miniskirt, jacket, and black knee-high go-go boots with a short heel. I remember thinking that her long brown hair looked healthy, and the crown of her head sunk into a huge floppy hat. When her gait placed her directly in front of the passenger seat I occupied, she stopped, turned, and stared at me through the car windshield. I stared back. Neither of us let our eyes go until she had crossed the street. We only broke our gaze when she needed to see where she was going. Two blocks down I said to my friend who was driving, "Did you see that girl?" He had noticed, and wondered what was happening. Did we know each other? Why hadn't I said anything? "She's a junkie," I said. There was a moment of recognition between she and I, and her stare felt like a challenge.

Last summer, after working night shifts at one of the smaller clubs on Broadway, a small group of us—dancers, DJs, and managers—would unwind at an apartment that two dancers shared. I was telling one of the managers a little about my past, and mentioned that I was attempting to write a dissertation on the sex industry. He asked me many provocative questions for which I had long rambling answers. Having earned his degree in photography at NYU only to find himself managing a strip club in San Francisco, he presented his story to me as an oddity that mirrored my own. There was a moment of recognition between us, and his questions felt like a challenge.

He wanted to know, from the perspective of someone who had attended graduate school in NYC, what the most surprising thing had been for me as a sex-industry worker. The doorbell rang. It was five in the morning and my cab was downstairs. I answered, "That it's so easy." It is so easy to become a whore. It is so easy to become a drug addict, to drink, to be touched for money, to gravitate in a world with complete confidence and clarity that in another life you might never have known existed. It is so easy to let the problems of the people around you become problems that you share, to find a social world that compels you simply because it is there, to sink into a world that is so easy to become a part of because all you have to do is show up.

"She's a junkie." To someone else that might mean that the girl I saw is simply a drug addict, and that that is all she is. For me, "she's a junkie" means that she has a social world that she gravitates within, that encircles her, a family that ties and binds with the liquid of heroin, which is just as reasonable a liquid to congregate around as blood. There is always the guarantee of shared interests, always the necessity of interaction, always the intensity of need and survival—all the things that congregations of shared blood can't promise, all the things that the families into which we are born have ceased to guarantee. The open road no longer seems that alluring, at least it holds little romance for most of the people I know, who express little interest in seeing the countryside. They travel the streets of the city instead shacking up in residential hotels, strip clubs, the places they get their drugs from (if they use), and their friends' apartments where they go to hang out after their night shifts end. The woman who crossed the street had a confidence about her; she wasn't a stranger in her surroundings, she could walk through a neighborhood that most people avoid, that many people only drive through because they're going somewhere else. She could wear her miniskirt, boots, and hat past all the men hanging out on the corners without being frightened, because they recognized each other. In her own social world, she had arrived.

SUBJECTIVE GLIMPSES AT ME AND THE MEN

At the start of every entry in my field journal is the following account(ing): Wednesday night—Name of club. Twenty-one dances/$650. Or: Sunday night—Different club. Fourteen dances/$390. This denotes where I worked, the night, the number of dances, and the amount made, which has inadvertently turned out to be a succinct and accurate predictor of the tone the accompanying passage will take. An entire multibillion-dollar industry erected on physical intimacy sold by the song. If you strip in San Francisco you might work at the Hungry I for stage tips and a portion of the fifteen-dollar drinks that the customers have to buy the dancers if they want the dancers to sit and talk to them; you split five of those dollars with the waitress and the house keeps ten. Or you might work at the Lusty Lady for an hourly wage, dancing in front of quarter-driven windows that rise and fall on the customers who jerk off in the tiny booths. Or you might lap dance. If you lap dance near Market Street you pay the club a stage fee that rises and falls with the vagaries of the industry, but typically settles around a hundred dollars.

If you lap dance on Broadway, where a single corporation has gobbled up every club on the block—from the biggest and most prestigious to the smallest hole-in-the-wall—you pay a stage fee that ranges between thirty dollars for a scheduled day shift and one hundred and thirty dollars for an unscheduled night shift, plus ten dollars to the house for every dance that you sell.

> Would you, could you dance on a man for money? *I would not, could not dance on a man, on a chair, in a club, sit on his lap and start to rub, on a couch, in a booth or bed, do you think I'm crazy in my head?*

Before you start dancing, the lap dancing part of it all seems like the hardest thing there is to do. Once you've worked for a while it can become the easiest. Mechanical or emotional, insipid or inspired, uncomfortably present or your mind drifting away, thinking about what you need to pick up at the store, effortlessly and unconsciously you subtly shift your weight in accordance with the erection beneath you. *With this dance I have nine and it's before ten o'clock, so hopefully if I make twenty I can finally pay off that fucking phone bill! Why am I such a long-distance queen? Oh shit, the song's over.* "Mmmm. You're so fun to dance with. Would you like me to stay?" My eyes stare into yours while we lie down on the bed "dance," my back turned to you as I grind on your lap "dance," a million styles of "dance," like butterflies in a glass case, all pinned down on a customer's lap—if they pay enough. If you work on Broadway, "enough" is well over the twenty dollars that management incessantly advertises as the one and only going rate for fully nude lap dances. An entire language steeped in subterfuge, gossip, and management-dancer quarrels revolves around making sure that you walk away from a dance with more than the ten dollars management reserves for you from a twenty-dollar dance. Generosity is appreciated; the more you pay the more I play; it can get hotter than that, much hotter; twenty dollars is the house dance, if you give me another one we can have a lot more fun—until you get fed up with it all and quote prices: twenty dollars I dance in front of you, forty dollars I dance on you, sixty dollars I rock your world. The management tells you that quoting prices is illegal because the mere mention of a figure transforms what we do into solicitation. The management thinks that we don't notice that the club quotes prices a thousand times a night. *That's right gentlemen, get that showgirl in a booth for twenty dollars, there's no reason to pay more.* Oftentimes the hardest part of the job can be getting the men to dance with you, and getting them to pay as much over twenty dollars as possible for their dance. Sometimes so much energy is expended on the sequence of events that leads up to the exchange of physical intimacy for financial compensation that the actual dance can pour through your muscles like a welcome relief.

THE CUSTOMERS

When a shift goes poorly I try to revive my inner warrior spirit who tells me that I will make money. I slip into my mantra given to me by a friend, "I am beautiful, I light up a room. There is no one here like me." I have yet to resign myself to the fact that I will have shitty nights now that I work on Broadway. So I pound my head against the concrete wall of customers saying no, no, no, again and again. Why won't these assholes sit with *me*?? Sometimes I take it very personally and circle amidst the customers like a hungry shark, certain that food and sustenance lay somewhere in the waters of the club. I hunt inert targets, sensing their uneasiness each time I circle around the stages. A customer at the ATM machine has spilled blood in the water and, all my senses alert, I approach with gaping jaws, hoping to snap hold of an ankle or wrist with enough bite to drag the body downstairs to my underwater lair—the "jungle room."

Sometimes, on one of those absurdly slow weekend nights when I'm sharing my shift with thirty-eight girls, my mantra doesn't work. The club becomes saturated with the uneasy lack of commercial exchange as the dancers circle the men, repetitively, desperately, asking for dances. With each new wave of frantic pleas "for company" you can watch them shrink into the oversized fluorescent drink cups they're pelted with after paying their admission fees. When there are that many girls working, and too few men spending money, it's hard to find your groove, to feel special, to not have your confidence shaken. On overcrowded weekend nights the ratio of rejection can skyrocket upward of sixty to one as the evening wears on. It becomes depressing and disorienting to mill through the crowd like a stale piece of meat. Everyone gives way to hysteria. Everyone's experience of having a bad night conflates until there is one master narrative of desperation that seems impenetrable. It's too hard to keep your hopes up, to think positive, to smile, to believe—the weight of so many girls not making money in the face of their expectations of how much money they should be making encircles you and convinces you to seek out the dressing room like a bomb shelter. On particularly bad nights even the DJs sink into the thick air of desperation, pointedly grumbling over the mike to the unappreciative audience surrounding the main stage, "I want to go out to a strip club and talk to my friends instead of watching the dancers. I want to go out to a strip club and sit in the corner and frown. I want to go out to a strip club and make sure that I don't get within one hundred feet of any naked women. I want to go out to a strip club and have a really bad time."

Some nights are uneventful except for the fact that I am tired, hungover, or have PMS, and inexplicably start crying over things that should have long ago become rote. On one such night some guy came in his pants and didn't tell me, and I didn't realize what had happened until I noticed a faint wetness on my leg. He refused to apologize, and simply commented "So what? This is your job." So I sat in the dressing room scrubbing my leg with a baby wipe while tears ran down my face. I kept saying over and over like a mad woman, "men are just filthy nasty disgusting pigs. I hate them." One dancer who I had never spoken to before came over to console me. I told her that I'm not naive, it was just the wrong thing to happen at the wrong time. She was having a shitty night, and was upset because she was trying really hard to make money but still couldn't get any men to dance with her. I actually did reasonably well financially, but the shift was hopelessly mired in the trough where the pigs feed. Not long after my first "disgusting man" interaction I had another with a customer who refused to give me anything over $20 for a dance. Moments after starting, he asked if he could kiss me, which resulted in my exasperated, unequivocal "no" while reiterating, for the second time, that he had to keep his hands at his side. The third time that he reached for me I used both of my hands to restrain his own, and he jerked forward like a baby rattlesnake striking out for a kiss. I ran out of the booth, him following me, unfazed by my disgust, indignantly pleading that the song wasn't over. I yelled at him. He muttered something indicating that he understood as he shrugged away. I almost felt bad for a second; he seemed truly hurt by my reaction. Our lips had only barely touched for a fraction of a second, but I couldn't tolerate one additional interaction with someone who was trying to get something that they refused to pay for, much less someone who was trying to take something that was not for sale.

Some nights are uneventful except for the fact that I'm rested, have a sense of humor, and everything turns out exactly the way I imagine it always should. Unfazed by rejection, unblinking in the bright lights, swaying with the music, strolling through the club, a genuine smile plays across my face, one that doesn't tremble in the corners of my mouth from the force of keeping my cheeks back. A good night for me, financially and emotionally, is when I sit for a small number of men who each buy a large number of dances. When someone buys ten forty-dollar dances from me, I've not only made three hundred dollars take-home pay in twenty-five minutes, but I've been spared all the work and aggravation that it would otherwise take to get ten separate customers to buy one dance a piece. When this happens at the start of a shift the whole night unfolds before my eyes bearing nothing but promise. Suddenly all the men seem polite and generous. I remember all of the compliments directed toward me and they make the intended impression—gorgeous, beautiful, elegant, princess. There are times when everything about a shift is perfect from start to finish—customers who adore you and kiss your hand good-bye before they leave the club, effortlessly impressive stage shows; it can feel like you have some kind of magic at your fingertips. When all the girls are making money, and the club is making money, it can feel like there's a complete synchronicity between the management, the customers, and the dancers. An unbelievably smooth operation measured throughout the night in the space of three-minute songs.

Some nights are eventful. The surrealism of your environment has the potential to flush you into unplungeable depths that you never imagined spinning in. *How do girls work in this club night after night over the summer?* Two-for-Tuesday at one of the smaller clubs on Broadway: if customers buy one dance they get the second dance for free. At this particular club that translates into four songs in the "fantasy rooms" upstairs, which is the equivalent of being slowly roasted in a brick oven, or jogging in the desert at high noon. In keeping with the miserable night I had two nosebleeds from overexhaustion and heat. When I got a chance I went into the slightly more bearable overcrowded dressing room to reapply the makeup I sweat off during the dances and tried not to puke. Room-temperature water made me feel sick, cold soda made me feel sick, eating, not eating, sitting, standing. Miserable. I made most of my money from three customers. The first kept asking me out to dinner. The second customer, more of an idiot, kept repeating his hotel and room number over and over like a subliminal recording. *Oh well, I really don't have anything better to do tonight, maybe after I soak my body in ice for an hour, scrub the layers of makeup off my face, tie back my wet greasy hair, shower away my exhaustion and grime, all the while tilting my head back to stave off future nosebleeds, I'll show up at your hotel and fuck your brains out.*

Before the dawning of my third customer I could already feel myself starting to crack. I met him during my last shift at one of the other clubs on Broadway, where he, always on the cusp of buying a dance without ever actually purchasing one, successfully manipulated time and attention out of me again and again, against my will and better judgment. And now he had come back to torture me some more, because I had told him I would be here. I don't think he liked the club or my dress. He asked me why I thought people sit with me. Too tired to talk, I told him that it was because I was sexy. He agreed that I was sexy, but that it was more than that, that he didn't know how to describe it, but that there was a heaviness about me, a heaviness that was slightly dark, substantial, real, and that you could see it when I was onstage. He told me that I should learn to accept that I have a sadness about me. I should have told him to fuck off and leave but I didn't. I felt trapped in this nightmarish hustle that I wasn't equipped to deal with. We finally danced after I poured attention on him for what seemed like hours. Then the scenario was repeated until I convinced him to dance again. Two-for-Tuesday. I don't know what I was thinking. In order to ascend the staircase twice to the fantasy room that bit like fire, I allowed myself to become entangled in a twisted two-day erotic scenario with a total stranger. I wanted everybody to save face, him thinking that I might have genuine interest in him, me actually giving dances to this guy that I told people had come from the other club to see me, I don't know.

It became a very confusing situation for me, the confusion apparent in the fact that I felt drained and used, exactly how I think he wanted me to feel. By the time he finally left we were both emotionally frazzled by a situation that had a "heaviness" about it well beyond the routine, but the bottom line is, I suppose, that he walked away this evening spending eighty dollars and I walked away earning eighty dollars. The bottom line is that when you tread water you don't drown.

THE MANAGERS

I adore and hate the managers in a fashion similar to the adoration/hate relationships I have had with male professors—men in positions of authority who have had the power to affect my lifeblood. Knowledge of the power relationships that exist within the clubs doesn't dry your eyes on a bad shift when the manager can be your salvation or your worst nightmare, just as knowledge of the power relationships that exist in academia doesn't dry your eyes when you've been ripped to shreds and a professor can be your salvation or your worst nightmare.

Sometimes a manager can become one of your best friends. One such friend asked me one night if he was a good manager. "Yes," I told him. Why? I told him that he seemed to have an understanding of what it is that we actually do, how our work shift doesn't feel like an assembly line to us, what a tenuous grip we can sometimes have during a shift, how, much physical and emotional energy it takes to sustain each lap dance, how when we have a bad dance, or a customer touches us inappropriately, or some idiot calls us a whore, or if we had a fight right before work with a significant other, all of these things affect our ability to work. I told him that his having a sensitivity toward and an understanding of the levels of intimacy in which dancers engage with customers when they're at work, and the difficulties that can surround engaging in such intimate interactions at work, can only help to create a safer working environment. I told him that he spares us the shit that passes for most manager pep talks—I can't just leave my personal life at home, I can't be insulted and or abused by one customer and just hop up unaffected to grab another, it matters if I'm tired, it matters if I did well or poorly the night before, it matters if I'm premenstrual, it matters, it matters, it matters. I told him that he allows himself to care about *how* dances are accrued for the club instead of just *how many*.

Some managers take their job very seriously. They might befriend you to a certain extent, but at work they are rarely your friend. Their job is to make sure that you make the club money. Their job is to collect that money at the end of the night. They barge into the dressing room to see what you're doing—*why do you need to put on more lipstick, they're just going to suck it off.* They watch your dances—*keep it clean in there*. The fact that the dance was clean and that your lipstick has never been "sucked off" is apparently irrelevant. These are just the things that they feel need to be said. The things that need to be said can often border on the bizarre. If I was in a funk, one manager would make me sit in his office until he felt he had revived me. He would always wait for me to talk first. I didn't always know what to say, so I would try to explain to him why I was having a bad night. I would try to produce information for him that would hopefully make clear to him by the end of our conversation that I had said what he felt needed to be said. One time I told him that I needed twenty dances, though I don't really know why I told him that. He asks, "Do you agree that I know everything?" He repeats himself until I say yes. He asks, "Do you agree that everything happens for a reason?" Again he repeats this phrase until I say yes. "Then go out there and get the dances," he continues, "because you know you can." On that magic note I was excused.

Some managers are evil. They use invasive psychological tactics for eight hours, and then wave to you at the end of the night with no sense of culpability for the tense, strained atmosphere they had almost single-handedly created. They have no idea what it takes to go in and do these dances, what we have to draw on, how hard we have to work physically and emotionally. They act like our fucking pimp and don't hesitate to take credit for our dance total at the end of the night. Their motivational philosophy is modeled on the image of an abusive husband, because verbal insults and the inconsistent deployment of "contract damages" for fucking up are the only things that "we" understand. Depending on my mood, it can take all of my strength to not pierce their throats with my stiletto heel to shut them the fuck up. If one of them approaches me I try to silently block them out. Wide-eyed I will myself to hear only the voice of Charlie Brown's teacher rambling on and on in the background. *I need to touch-up my eye shadow, change my outfit, and I don't get to have another cigarette until I've sold at least three dances*. He, of course, thinks that he's done something in those moments different than being an external irritant that has caused me to delve inward for composure. But even the evil managers have their favorites, forge bonds, and can surprise you with an act of generosity and compassion when you need it the most. Sometimes I wonder if the good, indifferent, and evil managers are the same for all the girls. Something tells me no.

One night at a smaller club on Broadway I got a gold star on my receipt. I asked the manager if I got the most dances and he said I was far and away the leader. I called my roommate at work the next morning to tell him. He said, "Talk about infantilization." Hmmm. That made me stop and think for a second, but I was still really happy that I got a gold star.

THE ACADEMIC COLLEAGUES

How do you let your male professor know that you've been a bad, bad girl? When I was in graduate school I was told that I was too theoretical, but I liked building things, playing a grown-up game of Legos with theoretical verses. But anthropology is about Real People in Real Places. I dropped out for a while. When I came back I started writing about people in places: *Sometimes the energy at the club is thick, you breathe it in as you walk around, cut through it sideways, hoping to part it in some way so that the air can propel you forward, which it can't. It's like working at a high altitude—hot humid and still. Your breath is short, each movement painstakingly wrought out of the lethargy that pins your arms to your side as you walk down the aisles, your lips in a frown when you ask for a lap, your ass in your seat when new men come in. Sometimes when you're on a lap and he breathes out and you breathe in, you can taste it, the same energy, shot in you, traveling through you. As the empty seats in the theatre slowly start to fill I can hear Elizabeth Taylor screaming in my ear, "Swampy, hey Swampy." It is like a swamp in here. If I stay just one minute longer I'll become a part of it, a Swampy, just like Richard, I'll be stuck in a swamp of pain and lies that revolve around a fictional child—the fiction being me here, my identity, more childlike as the months pass, more capable, each day, of swerving to miss a porcupine and smashing into a tree. I am not the only one who's afraid of Virginia Woolf.*

So, what have you been up to? *Oh, I don't know, dancing on men for money, cleaning up, treading water, the usual.*

I was told by a male professor whom I had considered a friend that my "so-called material" was worthless. He informed me that he had no interest in my people, in my places. He looked at me with disgust from his side of the desk. *You've been a bad, bad girl.* Then I met a new male professor "friend" who took an "academic" interest in me. Over coffee he would encourage a detailed account of lap dancing from me to the point of absurdity. *Just how bad of a girl are you?* I made painstaking efforts to detail for him instead the level of uncomfortability I had at the time disclosing such sensitive material to male academics, and the level of respect I would insist upon if we were to continue working as colleagues. I stopped returning his phone calls after he showed up unannounced to watch me dance naked onstage. He peered motionless from the second row through my entire set, and left without tipping. Sadly, whenever it comes to a quantity or quality of exchange where "value" in a cultural and Marxian sense is understood to be sexual in nature, everybody loses their heads. I'm supposed to feel the dirtiness and shame of what I do because otherwise intelligent people who are interested in issues of domination and oppression, specifically in celebrating and liberating the spiritual, intellectual, and material "value" of those who are dominated and oppressed, tell me that what I do is dirty and shameful.

My male friends who I went to school with worry about me and the men. Who am I when I exchange intimacy with strange men in three-minute intervals on an eight-hour shift for a negotiated amount of financial compensation? Am I an anthropologist? Am I a whore? How can I stand dancing for those men? It is sometimes difficult for me to explain to them that when someone gives me forty dollars to sixty dollars for sharing three minutes of my time with them I am grateful, happy, and feel a genuine kindness toward them, a genuine disposition to give them a good dance, to make them feel comfortable, aroused, intrigued, and, of course, desirous of spending more time with me at the same price. Working in the sex industry is, more often than not, exactly what it pretends to be. You give me money, I give you me. Sometimes simple, sometimes complicated. Sometimes I am self-conscious and watch myself trying to convince a potential customer that I am the best one for the job, that they should pay me instead of someone else to lay them back clothed on a bed, and drape myself over them with all the sexiness I can muster. I wonder where that girl came from. Perhaps I should worry more, but, for the time being, I make too much money to seriously consider swimming back.

2

The Phenomenology of Lap Dancing[18]

R. Danielle Egan

Phenomenology is the study of structures of consciousness as experienced from the first-person point of view. The central structure of an experience is its intentionality, its being directed toward something, as it is an experience of or about some object.[19]

Sexuality is one dimension of self, and a dimension which may be particularly challenged in the field, whether by the felt necessity for abstinence, the sexual temptations offered to us, the fears of professional consequences of sexual indulgence, and/or reactions of those we encounter to our perceived nature as sexual beings.

—Jill Dubisch[19]

Memory, like many things, is dynamic; it is prone to shift and change given new life situations, prone to partial forgetting and nostalgia. Five years distance from my time as an exotic dancer (and simultaneously, a sociology graduate student and researcher) provides me with both greater insight and a kind of memory loss about my experiences. Autoethnographic writing, however, requires a kind of coming clean that I have been able to avoid thus far in my professional work. Protected by my title as "sociologist," I could describe other dancers and even my own experiences in my writing, but due to style requirements and the norms of sociological texts, I could safely hide behind theoretical premises and specialized language. So although I might admit in public that "lap dancing was a complex interaction" dense with Lacanian classifications, I would never admit that, at times, I really enjoyed lap dancing, that it made me feel powerful and was pleasurable. Of course, there were also instances when I felt disgusted and even slightly nauseated. Or moments when I turned off—when my mind and body seemed a million miles apart—and just did the job. As such, this essay feels like another type of striptease where various protective academic layers get stripped away and leave me feeling more naked, or at least more vulnerable (due to the uncertainty of tenure decisions, my fear of feminist colleagues thinking I may not be dedicated to the cause or that my students may take me less seriously) than I ever felt onstage.

THE GIFT

While I gazed across the crowded floor of the strip club, devising my strategy for the evening, Sapphire[20] came up to me and said that she might have a customer for me. "He likes the intellectual type," she told me, "so I came and got you." As I approached his table, I did my thirty-second estimate of whether or not this man was a serious customer. A muscular white guy, in his late twenties with sandy blonde hair peeking out of his baseball cap, he sported the preppie uniform of khaki and olive green and introduced himself as "Colin." He did not seem stumbling drunk, was not part of a bachelor or fraternity party, looked like he could afford a few dances, and was pretty confident—all strong factors in the I-might-get-a-lap-dance-out-of-you-yet category. When I sat down he asked me my name and offered to buy me a drink. My confidence about the fiscal possibilities of our interaction quickly increased.

When the waitress delivered our drinks he asked, "So what do you do?"

"I'm a graduate student. What do you do?"

He evaded the question and the conversation stalled. Thinking my estimation of him as a profitable customer may have been wrong, I finished my drink just as he asked to go to the lap-dance room.

Amazed, I said, "Great, let's go."

While walking to the other room I heard him ask,

"Can I get your help?"

"Sure. Anything you want."

It was then that I realized Colin was blind. After leading him to a room surrounded by leather couches with women dancing and customers greedily trying to take in as much pleasure three minutes may afford, I situated him in the far left-hand corner of the room. We made small talk until the beginning of the next song. Unless you are with a regular, the few minutes before a lap dance begins are the most awkward, dancer and customer mumbling meaningless words in the hope of somehow magically erasing the fact that you are 1) in a public place, 2) with someone you hardly know, and 3) that you (the customer) are asking her (the dancer) to get nearly naked and grind against your lap for pay. Before our dance, I went over the rules, "You can touch my back or the bottom of my legs, but nothing else." Smiling, I added, "Now just sit back and relax." As the next song began, I took off my clothes and swiveled my hips, back, and butt against his legs and lap.

After about a minute Colin's hand traced up my back as he whispered, "You are so beautiful."

"Thank you."

"No, you really are beautiful."

"Thank you."

"You feel great."

"So do you."

"Let's go for another song."

"Great."

"You are so beautiful."

"Thank you."

This was the gist of our conversation. When I first started dancing I felt strange. A blind man telling me I was beautiful felt like other lies I had heard men tell me in the past, such as, "I am not seeing anyone else," or "You're all I need," but then something changed. Somehow I felt free of judgment about my body and was soothed by his words. It felt intimate and titillating. Of course, my mounting excitement might have had to do with the number of dances we were doing, after the eighth one I realized I was headed for an incredibly lucrative night, but I think it was something more. Performing without the judgment of his gaze gave me a sense of freedom. Released from worries such as, "Do I look sexy?," or "If I bend this way will my body bulge unattractively?" or "Why does he keep looking at me like that?" I could focus on the touch. His hand on my back, the cotton fabric of his pants against my leg, the feel of my satin gloves against my knees. Closing my eyes, I finished the dance in total darkness.

Merleau-Ponty, a French philosopher, argues against our culture's emphasis on vision because it perpetuates a gap between the person seeing and the person who is seen. Because of this gap, he believes that we often lose interconnection and the potential for mutual interactions.[21] To remedy this, he contends that we should foreground touch when thinking about the senses. In mutual and pleasurable touching, the connections between self and other can begin to change.[22] If we think about pleasant tactile sensation, it is hard to separate and figure out who is touching and who is being touched. The connection is less hierarchal and more interconnected. This is not to say that touching somehow negates the material inequalities and the complex way that power circulates in an exotic dance club, but it may help shed light on how, for that small period, I was able to forget that I was doing a job and shared a pleasurable sensual moment with Colin in the lap-dance room. My time with Colin is the example I give when asked by women, who mortified by my lap dancing ask, "Wasn't it horrible to have those men touch you?" Lap dancing was not always great, but it wasn't always horrible either.

THE T-SHIRT

Wearing a T-shirt with the words, "Like a Moth to a *Flame*" emblazoned under a row of bent-over nude cartoon women, I was a walking product placement for the club. Part of our job on

Fridays and Saturdays was to sell two club T-shirts and, although most of us thought they were tacky, lack of sales meant an extra forty dollars out of our pay.

Attempting entrepreneurial cleverness, I tried coming up with sales strategies, "Buy two lap dances and get this shirt half priced."

Or even better, "If you buy the T-shirt, I'll buy you a drink."

Working the room that night, all I could see were men surrounded by a sea of white T-shirt–clad dancers in Lucite shoes trying to hock the owner's garish brainchild. Customers were not buying and I feared I would acquire yet another two extra-large club T-shirts to add to my ever expanding collection and be forty dollars poorer at the end of the night. After several attempts, I came across Matt.

A twenty-something, athletically built, tanned guy in jeans and a white polo shirt, Matt loudly announced to his friends, after hearing my sales pitch, "Hey, I'm getting this shirt half-price and I'm getting off in the process." Walking into a room surrounded by an erotic assembly line of two rows of men sitting, not three feet from each other, on long couches with their hands by their sides while nearly nude or fully nude women danced the same moves for/on them, Matt staggered and I realized how drunk he really was. Sandwiched between two lap dances in progress, Matt asked, "You want to fuck?"

"No."

"Why not?"

"This is my job."

"Can I touch your pussy."

"No."

Reaching for my vagina, I caught his hand and moved it away.

"Come on."

Frustrated, I said, "Why don't you just enjoy your dance."

"Can I touch your breast?"

"No."

"I'm buying that fucking shirt aren't I?"

"Yeah."

"So can't I touch your pussy?"

"No."

Barely touching his lap and trying to avoid his grabbing hands, I whispered, "I really want to *dance* for you, but I can't if you keep doing this." After three or four professional attempts and getting thoroughly pissed off, I growled, "Do you want me to get a bouncer?" Finally Matt seemed to concede, "Alright, I will be good."

"Great."

Closing his eyes, Matt kept his hands on his lap until I turned my back to him. Encircling my body with his arms, he grabbed my crotch with one hand, pulled at my breast with the other, and proceeded to lick the side of my face. Feeling violated, but for some reason not wanting to make a scene, I whispered under my breath, "Get off of me." My paralysis felt like those times when strange men, approaching me on the street or in the gym command, "Smile," and somehow I compulsorily smile as opposed to saying what I really want, "Fuck off."

Furiously struggling to get free while he tightened his grip, I yelled, "Get the fuck off of me!" Louder still, "Get the fuck off me you fucking asshole!"

By then, other customers were starting to get up and come over to help, when I screamed again, "Bouncer!"

My voice cut through the music and two bouncers had him by his Polo and were throwing him out of the club, when I said, "Wait. He owes me money."

looked at the bouncers and said, "Fuck that."

anger, I demanded, "He owes me money!"

a bitch, a fucking cock-tease."

raised my voice, "This asshole owes me money!"

Assuring me that they "could handle it," the bouncers sent me down to the dressing room. Shaking and crying, I knew something in me changed. Later, Bryan came downstairs and gave me my money. Compensated for the dance and the T-shirt, I felt I had won a small victory.

Sex radical feminist Wendy Chapkis explains that sex workers are often subject to degrading comments and other forms of violence by those who view female sex workers as "fallen" or subhuman.[23] Given the cultural preoccupation with the control and regulation of women's sexuality, women who fall outside of prescribed sexual norms are given little cultural protection and support. When women mix eroticism and money, they violate cultural ascriptions of the inalienable connection between sex and emotion. Perceived as cold and calculating, sex workers are seen as duplicitous, abhorrent, and deviant.

Clearly, operating under these assumptions, some men treat dancers as easy targets. Unable to see me as anything other than a tool for his pleasure, Matt thought he could do what he wanted, when he wanted. I could have been anyone or anything (another dancer, a plastic doll, or a pornographic photo). The club became a place where his aggression against women was acceptable (although I would bet his misogyny was expressed in other contexts, too), because I was viewed as less than other women. Fitting me into the cultural classification of "whore" or grouping me with "the women you sleep with" instead of "the women you marry," he tried to make my body a means for his end. My fighting back, forcing recognition, and getting paid interrupted his simple vision of the world. After my experience with Matt, I felt more powerful and in control both inside and outside of the club. I got more assertive and little-by-little felt the yoke of bourgeois manners and good-girl behavior fade away. The effects of our encounter on Matt remain less certain.

THE PLUMBER

Sitting close to the stage, drink in hand, wearing a stained T-shirt that barely fit over his "beer belly" and a pair of sweat pants, he looked like the "cabaret type." Cabaret-only customers are men who try to get away with paying a lower rate (two dollars) for repeated "minidances" (normally used to entice men into twenty- to forty-dollar lap dances) on the main floor instead of paying full fare for a lap dance in the back. Most often cheap and obnoxious, dancers avoid them. Walking past his table, I did not smile or try to get his attention and was shocked when he said, "Hey, Kayla,[24] come here." In the end, fiscal need outweighed my desire to feign deafness and keep walking.

Sitting down at his table, before I could say anything, he ordered another beer, got me a drink, and told me his name was "Lenny." After his first swallow of beer, he asked, "What do you do outside this place?"

"I'm a student."

"Nice."

"How about you?"

"I'm a plumber."

"Great."

"You got a nice ass."

"Thanks."

"How about a lap dance?"

Glad that my assumptions were wrong, I said, "Great."

Finishing his beer, he got up, took my hand, and we headed toward the lap-dance room. Readying himself, he adjusted his pants, pulled his shirt over his stomach and got comfortable. After which, he looked at me and asked, "What is your name?"

"Kayla."

"No, your real name?"

I hated this question and often lied to customers who weren't regulars. Giving out my real name felt like a gift, an intimate gesture that he had not earned.

Trying to come up with a plausible name, I uttered "Gina."

"Yeah. Okay."

Affecting a seductive pose, I leisurely took off my red velvet gown in hopes of shortening my time on his lap. Afraid that his sweatpants would mean an orgasm I would literally have to *feel* (a truly disgusting, albeit not too frequent, cost of lap dancing), I stalled as long as possible.

The tactile nature of lap dancing separated it from any other part of my job at the club and involved a whole different level of emotions. Like when I was embarrassed and slightly pissed off at a customer who orgasmed about a minute into a lap dance and afterward, red-faced and confused, blurted out, "This has never happened before." Smiling and patting his shoulder, I said, "It's okay," even though his action meant another trek to the dressing room to pull out baby wipes and repress what I had cleaned off. Conversely, I got nervous when someone attractive sat on the couch and I felt his erection straining his Levi's against my leg, causing me to shift positions—it was always strange for me to dance for someone for whom I felt attraction (it was just too confusing). Or if some particularly repellent man asked for a dance, I held back a gag at the thought of smelling his hot breath in my face and feeling his body respond to my movements. In contrast there were times when I felt bored and lap dancing was just a mundane aspect of the job. This was particularly true when I was with men who, robotlike, sat underneath me, hands at their sides, and I felt only the material of their pants scratchy against my thighs. No erection. No smile. No nothing.

Lenny smelled musty. His combination of dirt, body odor, beer, cotton, and Brut cologne reminded me of men from my neighborhood: working-class men, quiet and serious, dirt underneath their fingernails, the scent of their work (motor oil, gasoline, or some other industrial product) following them home like a trace that lingers even after a shower. The kind of men I stopped dating when I went away to college and later to graduate school. His scent prompted memories of early boyfriends and the backseats of cars and hesitation giving way to anticipation.

"Nice ass," was all he said as I backed onto his lap.

Some men like to talk during lap dances. They get stuck in nervous banter jumping quickly from one topic to the next, in the hopes of creating a kind of hyperintimacy or hey-we-are-really-getting-to-know-one-another while engaging in a sensual act for pay. Lenny, on the other hand, said almost nothing. Occasionally grazing his hand across my backside, he smiled and said, "Let's do another" at the end of every song.

Dancing for Lenny was a powerful sensual experience. Without the distraction of conversation, I got lost in my own bodily sensation, moving in ways that turned me on. Lenny did not seem to care what I did and kept on buying. Every time I looked at his face, however, I got confused. How could I find someone that looks like this so erotic? How could *he* turn me on? He looked like the kind of guy I avoided and ignored at bars, but something about him affected me. Not grabby or rude, he seemed more interested in viewing my pleasure than in "getting his," and in so doing opened up a space where I explored a different kind of eroticism—mine. Body working against rationality, some strange confluence of nostalgia and autoeroticism unfolded that evening. At the end of our time, Lenny paid me and asked, "You gonna be here next week?" Happily, I replied, "Yep." As he walked away, I said, "My name is Danielle." He smiled and told me he would see me soon.

Lenny became my favorite regular.

Merleau-Ponty, in his philosophical musings, argues that our understanding of the world is an embodied practice.[25] He asserts that we experience the world through our bodies (as opposed to only our mind), particularly through its sensations and perceptions. When we touch or are being touched we are producing knowledge that helps us understand our reality. This knowledge can be painful in the case of nonconsensual or violent contact or pleasurable with mutual touching. In mutual touching, bodies become subject and object simultaneously. Control becomes hazy, undermining the power relations inherent in traditional subject/object divisions. When this happens, new understandings of the world become possible. In my first dance with Lenny, hesitation and disgust gave over to something altogether different—eroticism. Disgust and desire, after all, are linked in complicated ways.

Unlike the moments when I feel I cannot tell where my skin stops and my partner's begins—a feeling I often get when I am in love with someone—with Lenny there was a generosity between us where both bodies served the others (as opposed to one serving the other) and a kind of mutual autoeroticism blossomed. It was not the stuff of poetry (though I suppose it depends on the poet), but it was delightful.

THE CONFERENCE

Boarding a plane heading south for a conference where I was to present a paper on desire and power in exotic dance clubs, I realized how much I missed dancing (it had been just over two years) and was stunned by my yearlong absence from any exotic dance club. After a successful panel with two friends, one a former dancer and the other a regular customer, we decided to check out the scene in this small southern city.

Ravens, an amalgamation of exotic dance club and singles bar, had more women customers than I had ever seen before. Straight men, straight women, bisexuals, and lesbians intermixed more comfortably in this club than anywhere I had seen north of the Mason-Dixon Line. Laughing and drinking, inhibitions down, all seemed to partake in tipping and getting lap dances equally. The hedonism expressed in the club seemed closer to Paris in the 1920s than a small southern city in the middle of the Bible Belt and Bush country.

Dancers walking the floor gave mini-lap dances to male customers in the hopes of enticing them into a lap dance in the back. In their interactions with women, dancers employed a combination of erotic stimulation for the female customers and titillating spectacle for audience members. Slightly red-faced, female customers would sit with dancers straddling their laps. Dancer and female customer intertwined in these exchanges, which ended with the female customer's skirt at her waist with a dancer on her knees, "buzzing" the woman's underwear (a move we later learned was quite pleasurable).

From our seats, we watched a preppy girl get a lap dance, timidly at first. Halfway through the song, she pushed the dancer onto the floor, onto her back, and straddled her forcefully. We watched a girl approach the main stage with a dollar and get treated to a floor show far more explicit than any of the men had. The encounter ended with a deep kiss. As customers, we were becoming intrigued.

Simultaneously turned on and anxious, my friend and I ordered drinks. Spending a large amount of time and money previously in strip clubs, I was familiar with what it meant to be a customer; however, this was the first time I felt the deep pull of its seduction. As "Dakota" climbed the stairs to the stage, I thought she was beautiful. Short brown spiked hair, voluptuous curves in black tight shorts and a black leather bikini top, she seemed catlike onstage. Approaching her, dollar bills in hand, Dakota brought me onstage, lifted my shirt and kissed my chest. Walking back to my table, slightly dazed, I remember wanting more time with this woman. I thought, I must get a lap-dance.

Anxiously, I looked for her when she got off stage. Busily moving from table to table, Dakota disappeared intermittently to the back room for lap dances. It seemed like ages before she came to our table, and when she did I asked for a dance. Going to the lap-dance room with her and my friend, I got swept up. Bodies moving together, it felt erotic, sensual, and sexual. Lines between consumption and emotion blurred as I was sure she felt something for me and that I was somehow different from the others in the room.

After my first dance with Dakota, the experiences of regulars crystallized for me on a bodily level. I felt as if I had crossed to the other side, understanding the seduction regulars told me about. I experienced the lure, I wanted something more, wanted something authentic. To this end, Dakota was great. She made me feel special, showed me attention and made me want to spend more money (all challenging skills dancers must learn).

In the midst of our second dance, shifting positions of customer and dancer, I admired her prowess and skill as a dancer. Longing for my dancing days, I wanted to dance for Dakota. Offering to pay to dance for her, she relaxed on the couch. Pleasurable and exciting, I loved dancing for her. Walking out of the club, I realized how much more fun dancing was when you weren't dependent upon it to pay your rent (there's a privilege in dabbling versus having to dance for dollars). Or as Lily Burana states, "Funny how much nervier you can be when [dancing] not for necessity but sport."[26]

The tangled and messy aspects of lap dancing always seem to get hidden when they are discussed on talk shows or in the newspapers by those who have never stepped inside a strip club and/or have only ever seen clubs as they are represented in the movies or on television. The sensual, confusing, problematic as well as contradictory expressions of lap dancing get absorbed into moralizing statements of "I could never do that" or "God, wasn't it disgusting to have to dance for all those men?" I do not want to romanticize lap dancing as some panacea of gender equality under black lights—far from it—but lap dancing often moves beyond easy distinctions of good and bad, exploitation and liberation, moralizing disgust or pornographic representations of orgasmic delight.

The point is that lap dancing evades easy description.

Lap dancing illuminated the complicated ways in which pleasure, pain, and gender could intersect. Yearning intertwined with capital to reveal the similarities of financial and emotional need: wallets opening and closing based on both emotional and erotic seduction, regular and dancer vacillating between positions that almost never produced easy hierarchies.

Like some customers who found themselves caught in the tangled web of desire and disgust, desperately wanting what a strip club could offer in the lap-dance room but embarrassed or disgusted by their bodily responses (erections and/or orgasms) or even by the women who provided those responses, lap dancing poses paradoxes not easily resolved.[27]

3

The Grind

Susan Bremer

Who are you?" I demand of the thin man bent over boxed rows of CDs in the corner of the long narrow room. I can barely see amid the dark shadows of the DJ booth but this person's outline is different from that of anyone I'm accustomed to. My eyes haven't adjusted to the poorly lit cubbyhole yet and, as he turns I see buzzcut hair and a nose ring. The other DJs have long hair.

"Randy," he says.

"You're new. How long have you been here?" I've been working at the club since opening night two and a half years ago and consider it my right to know everyone.

"One week."

"I've been gone for a week. Where's the other DJ?"

"They all quit."

"All quit? All three of them?"

"Yeah, the owner wanted them to take a pay cut," he says as he pushes past me to get to the microphone.

The strobe and many colored neon light controls, dual-decked CD player, and microphone are situated in a recessed corner to the right of the doorway I walk through. The window behind the electronic controls makes it easy for the DJ to look down upon the stage and the main floor of the club.

"Okay let's give it up for Heidi," his voice booms into the microphone and throughout the building. "She puts on one great show and is now available for that up close and personal VIP dance. Next to the stage is that tempting Tootsie from Texas. Let's welcome up Tootsie." Turning to me without taking a breath he continues, "They all quit on Friday."

"Oh," I say aloud. Saddened by the news of losing Tom, Steve, and Trevor, DJs who'd been with us since opening night, I retreat from the booth and descend the stairs to the main floor. On my way to the dressing room I stop to say hi to Virginia and drink a cup of coffee while she smokes her cigarette.

"Crowd's pretty thin," she tells me. "Oh by the way, we now have funny money."

My sadness quickly turns to anger, but I don't want to be angry. Getting mad means less tips for me. "I'm not going to think about it," I tell her, "I'm just going to come here, make my money, and leave."

But I can't stop thinking about it. In the time I've worked at the club I've seen our fees escalate from twenty to fifty-three dollars a night. And with funny money (paper money given to customers that they purchase on their credit cards) the management could now take another ten percent of our earnings automatically when we turned the fake bills in for cash. The club isn't getting any busier either—in fact, the clientele has dropped off and with thirty to fifty women on the schedule each night the struggle to make money is getting tighter and tighter.

They call us "independent contractors" and charge us a stage fee, the premise being that we're using their stage to advertise ourselves, so we pay them. All the clubs work this way. Our money comes solely from the customers. Each night we dance onstage for a two-song set while the patrons tip, usually only a few bucks. When we're not onstage we circulate throughout the club mingling with customers, engaging them in conversation, and asking if we can dance for them. The bulk of our money is made by doing personal dances. The men sit in their chairs while we stand in front of them, remove our dresses, and dance in bikinis for one song. For these dances the men pay ten or twenty dollars depending where they're seated in the club; the main floor dances are less expensive than the VIP level, which advertises a more intimate and relaxed atmosphere.

A boyfriend once referred to me as the consummate professional. Every night, alone in the pit I duke it out using an arsenal of luminous charms, colossal smiles, fetching eyes, gallant flattery, toned muscles, breath-freshening mints, and business savvy. In this highly competitive, each-woman-for-herself environment, some make hundreds, some make enough to squeak by and keep coming back, and some lose money. In most jobs, if you're a little depressed, in a bad mood maybe, you can still function at work and depend on that paycheck, but as a dancer, being depressed can severely limit your income. The perky invitation, "Hi, would you like a dance?" is undermined by glum eyes and a mild smile.

Attitude is everything.

Carrying my coffee and backpack crammed with evening attire and makeup, I walk downstairs to the dressing room.

"Do you think I need a face-lift?" Juanita asks.

I laugh, "Juanita you're only twenty-six."

Morgan offers, "Yeah, if you get anything, maybe you'd like to have your nose done like me."

Madeline, a muscular former ballerina, current wife, and mother, who's very private and doesn't usually get involved in dressing-room chatter, walks in, gives her fifty-three-dollar stage fee to the housemom, and leaves to get ready in the other dressing room.

Peaches walks in and gives me a hug.

"How was your final?" I ask.

"I got an A," she beams. Peaches has been out of high school for four years and is now taking general prerequisites at the local college.

"I knew you could do it," I tell her, "Congratulations." Her electric green tube top and matching skirt are screaming at me. "Is that a new outfit?"

She nods. "It's my present to myself for making an A."

Doreen, a tall brunette with big brown eyes and new size "D" breasts, which aren't too large for her well-proportioned body and hips, is talking about her first teenage sexual experience. "We never even got to the sex part. We were just kissing and touching, it was really hot, and then he got stuck in his zipper. That kind of broke the mood."

We all laugh.

I enjoy the camaraderie with the women, the way we call each other "baby" and "sweetie." We hug and pat each other's bare butts and occasionally even squeeze another woman's breast, to see if her "job" feels real. We share makeup, nail polish, and clothes. In the dressing room there is no competition.

Candy walks in. I've known Candy over three years and she's my idol. When I first started dancing and didn't really know what to do, I watched her. Candy is always sensuous, and she makes a lot of money. It isn't that her body is anything extraordinary; she's a short woman with a layer of baby fat, but she's rounded in all the right places. Candy has a way of mesmerizing men with her facial expressions and slow fluid movements. I studied her and perfected the moves in my own dance. Candy and I maintain the dance in its original choreography, an art form of tease and seduction.

Candy is so successful at this art form she keeps the men returning for years. One customer bought her a car and another invested money in stocks for her. No man suspects she's in a long-term, monogamous, lesbian relationship.

I finish getting ready and ascend the stairs to survey the happy-hour crowd.

Five men sit at a table watching the stage where an extremely tall, model-thin black woman is dancing topless. She must be on the second song of her set, the only time when we women are topless in the club. Because our club sells alcohol, local law dictates that we stay at least six feet from the customers when we have bare breasts. One of the men approaches the stage with a one-dollar bill, she sways over to him, covers her breasts with her arm, holds out her bottom strap where he places the bill, says, "Thank you," and moves away from the railing.

Which one should I approach? The first conversation of the night is always the hardest. They're all dressed in suits, have corporate hair, wedding rings, and two beers in front of them. I walk up to the man with the most relaxed appearance—legs extended casually in front, arms open at his sides, and a big grin on his face. He's the only one wearing a beard and a small diamond earring.

"Hi, my name is Honey," I whisper into his ear. My right breast presses against his left arm to pique his interest and my lips almost touch his ear so I don't have to shout over the loud music. My throat has been hurting lately.

He turns, smiles, speaks, and I note his breath—beer and cigarettes. His name is Bill, or so he says. Some men adopt stage names just as we women do.

"Would you like a mint?" I ask, producing a pack of Altoids from my purse, popping one into my mouth, and punctuating the sentence with, "Not that you need one." I don't want to offend.

He launches into all the lines I've heard before: "Honey? Bet your mother didn't name you that, what's your real name?"; "You sure look sweet enough to eat."; "You can spread on me anytime you'd like."

I giggle and use my high-pitched, childlike work voice. I widen my eyes and coyly angle my head to the side. Outside the club I'm straightforward in gaze and speech. I laugh a throaty, hearty laugh when I am not at work. In here I tittle and win him over.

When a new song starts, I rise, stand in front of him, and bring my head close to his so our noses almost touch. I flip my long blonde hair so it surrounds his head, a flaxen tent with our two faces as the only occupants. I hold his gaze like a lover in silent adoration while my brain calculates how much money I want to make this evening.

I straighten and remove my purple sequined cocktail dress. Over and over—thirty times a night if I'm lucky—I flip my hair and stare into their eyes. I shove my arched back and buttocks into their chest and face. I clutch their shoulders and bring my lips close to their ear. I sit in their lap and lean back against them, drawing my breasts together with tight arms to accentuate my cleavage. I dig my nails into their knees and look up into their eyes from my kneeling position at their feet.

A manager once said to me, "You make so much money."

It's true. An accomplished dancer can make anywhere from

two-hundred to many multiples above that, in cash, in one night. But what he didn't recognize are all the unfavorable situations I endure to earn that money. Imagine spending eight hours with a relative you don't like, trying to keep the conversation flowing when you're really not interested in talking. I tolerate strangers' alcohol breath and spit unintentionally spraying on me. I ignore, sidestep, or sometimes counter derogatory wisecracks, off-colored jokes, sexual innuendo, and verbal sparring.

Seated in front of me, Bill sighs, "You're killing me." He's trying to blow in my ear and touch my legs. "I'm really good with my tongue," he says and sticks it out and rolls it around. He keeps asking me to pull my bikini bottom to the side. "Just give me a peek, no one will see," he suggests. When the song ends I inquire, "Would you like another dance?" I have to ask, this is my job, but because of his bad breath and incessant pleading I don't care when he says, "No."

Sliding into a chair at a new table I say, "Hi, my name is Honey." His smile widens at me as he looks away from the stage. I perform this routine so much the words and phrases roll off my tongue like cards flipping on a fast-turning Rolodex. "Have you been in here before?" I ask.

"No, first time."

"Are you from out of town?"

"Yes, Dallas." He is still reserved, a little intimidated I suspect by the way he hugs himself.

"What do you do?" I ask.

"Lawyer."

"Are you here on business?"

"Yes."

"Well, its a good thing you stopped in here because I'm in the monkey business," I whisper.

His face lightens and he relaxes a little deeper into his chair. Laughing settles them down and warms them up.

"You're so beautiful," he tells me.

"Thank you. This really isn't my body, I just rent it. I keep it in a locker downstairs," I tease, bringing out all the lines that usually make them grin. His arms relax. It's time to close in.

"Can I dance for you? Not this song, it's already started, next one," I say.

"Not yet, I'm waiting for a friend."

I'm not taking "no" for an answer though so I bring out my next round of well-used lines.

"We could do a dance now and that way when your buddy comes you'll be able to recommend me."

"No, that's OK, but thanks. Why don't you come back when my friend comes in."

My demeanor changes from sweetness to subtle arrogance. "If I have time later I'll come back." Sometimes the men don't know how to say "no" and instead play the "maybe later" game. My fatigue level or how many times I've been put off in an evening determines my reaction to their rejection. I've learned that "maybe later" usually means never. I hope the club will be so busy I won't have time to return.

When I first started dancing I would sit for a long time with one man, listening to his anecdotes, waiting for the right time to ask for a dance. As my time in the business increased I learned how to feel the man out and intuit if he would spend money. I don't sit with them as long anymore, instead I chat them up quickly for a song or two and then ask, "Can I dance for you?" If they're not going to let me dance I want to know right away. If they are going to let me dance, they usually do it soon.

Some nights they're drawn to me: woman scent, pheromones,

alchemy, I can't explain it. At a fairly regular time in my menstrual cycle the men are most responsive to my advances. Stop at a table, talk for a few minutes, ask for a dance, shake breasts in face, leer into eyes, wiggle butt, put a little pressure onto lap, pantomime ecstasy, collect money.

Other times in my cycle I can't get a dance even if I pay them.

I continue circulating and meet Steve, a twenty-four-year-old apprentice stockbroker. He tips me sixty dollars extra and doesn't try to put his hands all over me. "I like older women," he says.

Two men are talking as I approach their table and chide, "You're talking business are you?" This usually gets them to admit they are, and then I can come back with, "I've come to save you from that," or, "Isn't it time to put the work away and have a little fun?"

These two are not that playful. I make a little small talk and sensing that they aren't going to bite, ask fairly soon if I can dance for them.

The man seated to my right hesitates and I prod, "What? What are you going to say?"

"Okay, I'm going to say this but you're not going to like it." I shrug. He continues, "I like a woman who is smart, fun, nice."

I break in, knowing I'm all of these things but realize this guy can't know that in the two to five minutes we've talked. "And you're saying I'm not?"

"Of course not, I don't know you."

"Exactly," I say.

"You see, I don't get dances. I think it's degrading," he offers.

"Then why are you here?" I ask as I glare into his long thin face.

"I didn't want to come. My friend dragged me," and he gestures to a man in the corner getting a dance from a slender brunette in a vinyl pink bikini.

"We're here by choice," I respond quickly. "No one's forcing us to be here," then I say, pausing for emphasis, "But you're the one who's here against his will."

"Yes, but . . ."

I don't give him a break, "It seems to me that you're the one being degraded because you're the one who's here under duress. Is that smart enough for you?" I walk away.

It is very important to keep positive energy and an "up" outlook all evening; one negative person can deflate a mood and ruin a whole night.

One night I sat on a loveseat in the VIP area waiting for the next song to start so I could dance for the man seated next to me. He was the embodiment of the corporate professional: tailor-made black suit and gold cuff links, perfectly manicured nails, exactingly trimmed brown hair and sideburns. Vodka emanated from his body and rimmed his eyes with red.

"I hate my clients. They're all stupid," he informed me.

I smiled.

"I know all dancers feel the same about the men in here: just poor saps with big dollar signs on their faces. That's the way I see my customers," he droned on.

I tried to tell him I didn't feel that way, that I actually liked most of the men, the ones who weren't rude or disrespectful, but he never heard me. As I sat staring with amazement at this not unattractive man I tried to forgive his dour antagonistic remarks. I wanted his money. I had cajoled and matched wits with him at the bar earlier and my reward was going to be the twenty dollars for a dance.

But he wouldn't shut up. "I'm in sales too and I always think, you poor suckers, after I close a deal. They keep making me money though and I laugh all the way to the bank."

"Are you saying that's how I feel about you?" I asked.

"No, not me, I'm really cool. You can see that," he preened. "The rest of those jerks: they come in here thinking you're going to fall in love with them and really you think they're pathetic. I do it, too. All the while I'm closing a deal with a customer I'm thinking, you schmuck. You're making me rich."

The clientele was minimal that night but I finally had enough of his hateful black spirit. I removed my arm from around his shoulder and stood. "I'm going to show you I'm different," I said. "I don't even want to dance for you." I walked away.

Walking away can help to keep the "up" attitude. There is nothing more satisfying or more liberating than walking away from some of the men. Even in a business where I want something from them I still can choose where to spend my time.

One evening I encountered one man right after another who wanted to play touchy-feely. (I don't know why but there always seems to be some kind of theme during a night. Sometimes I'll meet seven men named Steve, or seven attorneys, or all men from Chicago, or all men that want to touch my butt.) I walked away from two men in a row without getting any money because they wanted to maul me and I was in no mood.

The first man was extremely thin, sporting a long red beard, jeans, and a beer-stained flannel shirt. He had a pleasant demeanor and didn't appear drunk. The song began and I stood up to start the dance. Before I could even remove my dress, he grabbed my butt cheeks with both hands and held on tight. I laughed playfully, removed his hands, and continued dancing, trying to remove my dress. His hands next flew to my waist and up to my chest. I looked him in the eye and said sternly, "You can't do that."

"I'm paying you twenty bucks for one song, I'll do whatever I like," he said and grabbed for my crotch.

I hoisted the top of my dress back up, said, "We're done," and walked away. The next man I approached asked me right away if I'd dance for him. "Sure," I said cheerfully, happy to meet someone new and enthusiastic after the groper. But as soon as I had my dress off, the man was tugging at my bikini top and trying to touch my breasts.

"That's it!" I blurted. I grabbed my dress and stormed off.

It's not always an easy decision to walk away and I haven't always been so clear of my boundaries. The dilemma of what to tolerate, what personal boundaries to erect and enforce, always revolves around money. Tolerating or not tolerating invasive advances might make the difference between earning one hundred or three hundred or six-hundred or eight-hundred dollars in one night. It might make the difference between working four nights or two nights a week, dancing full-time or part-time.

"Why are you laughing?" the Buddha-shaped man asked.

"Because I'm having fun," I lied. Really I wanted to take his grubby little fat fingers off my skin, but something stopped me. He was inching over to cup my breast, trying to place his mitts on my nipples, and I giggled and slid away. But he had already copped a feel. Why was I letting him get away with this? I tried to block his advances by squeezing my arms tight against my sides and turning my back to him but then he grabbed my butt.

Seated in front of me this short round man with a balding head and pockmarked face was leering at me with I'll-pay-you-anything-to-sleep-with-me eyes. I knew those eyes—desperate, pleading. I repositioned my body but the Buddha was still trying to touch me. This time it was my scantily clad crotch. The thin white strip of my one-piece bikini covered the bare minimum.

He tried. I laughed.

After a few years in the business I developed enough confidence and experience to know that I could make money without compromising my personal boundaries, but these values are always being challenged by men who believe we dancers will allow *anything* for money. I'm confronted with the temptation of more money if only I'd . . . , on a daily basis. I dance and wiggle my bottom and breasts, and my new acquaintance, Harry, asks, "Can we make a deal for an hour?"

"A deal, what kind of deal?" Between the bartering and laughs, I deduced that this one, the Park Avenue guy from New York, wanted me to grind him to ejaculation. Then he would go home to his hotel and sleep.

"I don't think I can do that," I flustered, not wanting to forgo the several hundred dollars he was offering me, but also not wanting to commit to something I found repugnant.

"Use your hand a little," he said.

"I've never been asked this before." I couldn't believe what I was hearing. I had always worked in gentlemen's clubs that provided visual entertainment only, and the men, though asking me for many things, had always understood there wasn't such explicit contact.

"You're kidding, right?" he continued.

"No. No one has ever come out and asked me to grope him. It's a visual experience. I dance, you watch."

"I'm a nice guy," he said, and added as if I was a naive fourteen-year-old, "You won't get pregnant."

"I know that." These propositions are expected within the walls of the strip club, so I made allowances and didn't get angry.

I once had a man, a regular customer to some but I had never seen him, stay the entire evening with me, from 8 P.M. until closing at 2 A.M. We sat upon a couch, drinking and talking like we were on a date; he, a short thin man with receding black hair and black plastic glasses, wearing gold cuff links, a gold watch, and a blue-striped power suit and I, an attractive blonde woman wearing a pink spandex cocktail dress and faux diamond and sapphire rings. I danced some and talked some. If we were on a date though I wouldn't have been taking off my dress and shaking my barely covered breasts and butt in this well-respected, international businessman's face. If we were on a date he wouldn't have been paying me money to stay with him. When his money ran out, he went to get more from the ATM. He came back and told me he had reached his ATM limit for that day and wanted to know if I trusted him. Would I stay with him and the next day he would pay me double what I usually made. He gave me a small diamond ring he was wearing as collateral. Hesitant but intrigued by his offer of double pay and too tired to mingle with the other customers, I said I would stay. We continued the evening as he drank bourbon after bourbon and professed his affection for me.

"Would you like to have dinner?" he asked. "In New Orleans." We were sitting in a club in San Francisco. He offered shopping sprees and luxurious evenings.

As the DJ announced that the club was closing he looked at me sheepishly through his glasses, held my hands in his and said, "I lied. I wanted to test you, see if you were loyal, really interested in me."

I have your ring, I thought.

He had been able to get money from the ATM earlier in the evening when he'd said he couldn't. He gave me more of what he owed but it wasn't the full amount so I kept his diamond ring and he promised he'd be back the next day. When I didn't see him for two weeks, I became concerned. Another dancer who knew him told me he was out of town so I relaxed some, but I still had the ring appraised at a pawnbroker to see what it might be worth. Not enough. Inwardly I fumed. When he finally returned I collected my money (not the double pay he had promised) and I have never talked to him again.

But it's not just the customers who try to take advantage of our working bodies.

The club receives its money from the door cover charge (twenty dollars), the drink prices (five dollars for a small cup of coffee), and the dancers (our stage fee of fifty-three dollars). The DJ, and the housemom (the woman who makes schedules and supplies items for the dancers such as tampons, nail polish, no-slide shoe pads, hair spray, and chocolate), are also charged a percentage of the dancers' earnings. We'd gotten new carpet and couches, but we hadn't seen advertisements for the club increased. I hadn't seen the ATM fixed and it had been broken for six months. I generated a petition outlining the club's as well as the dancers' monetary benefits from having a working ATM, all the dancers signed it, and we faxed it to the owner. He agreed that we needed to have it fixed but instead of a consistently working ATM the customers could use (and from which we could keep all of our earnings), the club decided to take 10 percent more of our earnings by having customers use their credit cards to purchase "funny money" from the cashier. Now, approximately ten months later, we finally have a working ATM—a working ATM that *only* dispenses funny money.

One club I worked at allowed customers to purchase dance tickets on their credit card for thirty dollars a ticket. The men then gave the tickets to the women for personal dances. At the end of the evening the club reimbursed the women fifteen dollars for each ticket and kept records of each dancer's earnings. At the end of the year the club issued a 1099 that documented each woman's ticket money for the IRS wherein the club credited her with the full thirty dollars for each ticket instead of the fifteen she actually made. One dancer complained to management that she hadn't made that much money. They fired her. But technically they can't fire someone who is not an employee so they just said she couldn't come back.

Ten dollars of the house fee the club charges is used for a promotional review. The women are required to buy a shirt for ten dollars and during the promotional review it's the dancer's responsibility to sell the item. She offers a dance and a shirt for twenty dollars. Whether she sells the package or not she's out ten dollars. Some women have a whole closet full of shirts.

Tonight, the next man I meet after "Mr. Aren't You Degraded," is Tom, a psychology professor giving a lecture at Stanford who is slight of build with a receding hairline. I feel relaxed with him and talk longer than my usual five minutes before asking for a dance. As I dance for him he speaks lovingly of his wife who he's been married to for twelve years. He doesn't stare at my body parts like many men do. He only wants to talk but realizes I'm here to make money so I dance two songs then sit and talk for two songs, then repeat the cycle of dance and talk. We spend an hour discussing the Midwest, family life, his two young girls, and the cultural differences between the East and West coast. He enjoys the clubs because as he travels the United States he finds himself in strange cities with time on his hands. When he gets ready to leave, I give him a hug, wish him and his family well, and go off to meet someone new.

I see Lenny sitting by himself at the right side of the stage. I walk up to him, my arms engulfing, my smile as wide as the Cheshire Cat's, "It's so nice to see a familiar face," I say.

"Honey, I was hoping to see you tonight. The last few times I've been in you weren't here. I was wondering if you'd quit," he says, exuding enthusiasm.

We embrace each other in a bear hug.

"No, I'm still here. Only working a few days a week though. College keeps me pretty busy."

I sit talking with him awhile because we've known each other for three years and it feels good to catch up. Lenny's not an attractive man at first glance, but his personality and genuine respect are large enough to make him and his short stocky frame, acne-scarred face, and large round nose and glasses disintegrate into a charming child. When I dance for him he takes his glasses off and I see into his bottomless aquamarine eyes.

After I dance for Lenny a couple of songs, I dance for a few unfamiliar faces and then take a walk upstairs to see if there are any new customers in the VIP area.

"Honey! Honey!" I hear as I start making my way to the DJ booth. A hand is swiftly on the small of my back and I turn around. It's a familiar face—but I can never remember his name. He's been in numerous times, is from Seattle, and is a generous spender.

"What a nice surprise," I say truthfully. I know that for the rest of the evening, two hours until club closing, I'll have good company, interesting conversation, and financial reward. Dancing in the club is a business. I offer a service of company and entertainment. I expect to be paid. When men try to quibble about money or tell me, "I don't believe in dances," I ask them, "What do you do for employment?" I also remind them that if all the men coming into the club thought like they did, they wouldn't have a place to watch the women dance onstage because we wouldn't be able to afford to work. Sometimes a man will offer to pay for a dance for his friend. Sometimes, the friend, for whatever reason, intimidated, shy, nervous, or having a loving wife at home, will decline the dance saying, "That's okay." At this refusal I am quick to say, "Do it for me, I need the money." Many of us would like the men to remember this. Most of us are not in the club because we want to find a boyfriend, a husband, or a dinner date. We are not there because we enjoy unfamiliar men touching or leering at us. We might have psychological issues that keep us coming back—like actresses, we may come to crave the attention and adulation—but the biggest draw is the money.

I have to pay the club if I want to work. And I have to cater to the customers in order to get my money from them, just as I had to cater to engineers, physicists, and managers when I worked in business and as a laser technician. I have flexibility and can easily travel the United States working in other clubs, finding clubs where the money is more plentiful, but I will never get a raise. I can only be sure that each place I decide to dance I will encounter the same dynamics. I want the men's money and the club wants mine.

I have a good act, the same five-minute monologue that I enact over and over to each new man. I perform for eight hours a night. I run my hands down my belly playfully hinting at masturbation. I run my hand along my inner thigh outlining my well-defined muscles. I suck on my finger.

By the end of the evening I'm drained; my feet hurt, my butt is sore from wearing a t-back bikini bottom that feels like having a wedgie all night, and my gaze into their eyes becomes shorter and shorter. For eight hours I listen to and laugh at their jokes. I hold their hands and massage their shoulders. I honestly share details of my life and dreams for my future. (Some women lie about themselves but I've never been able to.) I listen to their fantasies and insecurities about women. I hug them and wish them a safe journey.

At the end of the night I drive home in silence wearing comfortable jeans and a T-shirt—I'm ready to remove the makeup, take aspirin for my aching feet, and crawl under the electric blanket, alone.

4

The Lap Dancer and the "Business Man"

Shelly Manaster

Once upon a time in San Francisco, at a gentlemen's club on Broadway there were two "business men" who had been hanging around upstairs for an hour or two. By "business men" I mean a particular category of customer who chooses to present themselves in a particular way. Everybody is involved in business in one sense or another, at least everybody needs to earn a living, but the "business man" carries himself just a little differently, to convey the accidental motive behind his visual consumption of strip-club culture: he works down the street, his friends dragged him in, a deal was just closed that made the "business men" feel randy, wild, and on top of the world—what better way to celebrate than to pound a few vodka tonics and go look at naked women? While most men you end up sitting with wish you could be their wife, "business men" wish to make it clear from the start that you couldn't be their wife, that the fact that you dance naked in front of other "business men" is self-evident enough as an explanation as to why you are not girlfriend or wife material. They are the most adamant in resisting the lure of lap dances, they don't need to pay for attention, and tend to favor word-economy and rudeness to make this clear when you approach them. They tend to favor silicone breasts, g-string tan lines, and bleached hair, signs that the group can recognize together as constituting a sex-industry worker from years of exposure to *Playboy* pictorials. These breasts and tan lines can be treated badly. They are meant to be consumed. Those dancers who do not provide this visual stimulus do not even merit the attention of poor treatment. They are dismissed outright.

"Business men" "laugh at" while poorly pretending to "laugh with." "Business men" are looking for that special touch of Vegas vacation in their night out at a San Francisco strip club. The "business man" comes in after work wearing a suit, tie, and starched white shirt. He rarely travels alone, and tends to congregate in packs, although he can often be found in groups of two or three. Even in the club, he walks with the other "business men" of his group. They can usually be found inelegantly straddling the back wall in an attempt to give the impression that they are "at ease," or clustered around the main stage, usually from the second row back, so they do not feel as if they are required to tip. When the "business man" does tip, he moves with great effort from his seat in the third or fourth row to toss a dollar on the stage with much fanfare from the other "business men" who hoot and holler and pat him on the back. Sometimes a "business man" will remove his jacket and place it on the back of his chair; most, however, appear to feel more comfortable wearing their suits at all times. Sometimes the "business men" go to happy hour before the strip club, they are usually the ones who wish to give the appearance of being "at ease" because the intoxicants make their blood warm and their posture languid, and so they prop themselves against the back wall, which effectively blocks the passage of dancers trying to maneuver in the back aisle. The "at-ease business man" can then grab the dancers by the arm as they walk by and ask them what goes on in a place like this. He will entrap a girl in a lengthy discussion about pricing and activities, tell her he's not interested in having a dance yet, and then, upon her departure, immediately latch onto a new informant, asking the same questions. The "at-ease business man" can derive many hours of pleasure from performing this ritual over and over, until the girls start making a wide semicircle of passage around him. Only the true hustlers can, or would, snag him at this point, by grabbing or coercing him into a booth, gauging that after hours of hearing the same repetitive information he might be ready to spend some money.

Being a true hustler, I make the misguided decision to snag one such "at-ease business man" (who will herewith be referred to as Mr. Tie for the sake of brevity) on a Friday night and drag him downstairs for a dance. Before nine o'clock on Fridays, customers get a free dance if they buy two in a row, which is the package deal I try to sell to Mr. Tie. Mr. Tie wants to know if he can touch me here or there, pointing somewhat rudely, to which I respond, "No." *Why didn't I walk away? I always think I can handle these situations even though my little voice is telling me that the guy is a complete asshole; after all, I've made money from complete assholes before, none the worse for wear. Or am I?*

"Can I touch your pussy?"

"No."

"Why, wouldn't it feel so good? I could make you feel so good that you wouldn't want to charge me."

"Yes, well, nonetheless I'm at work, and what you're suggesting is illegal, and I could lose my job as well as be prosecuted."

"Who will know? I promise not to tell."

For some reason all "business men" have this same response, as if we can sniff out the blackness of their soul and if caught engaged in illegalities would somehow assume that they would be the one to blow the whistle. Doesn't it seem kind of redundant and stupid to ask me to engage in an illegality and to then inform me that they won't tell; wouldn't that just be assumed? Nonetheless this is always the first line out of their mouths: I won't tell; next, no one will know. You yourself apparently have no identity as a witness and no presence of recognizable authority over the limits of your own body because the fact that you will know always seems to perplex them when given as a response to the no-one-will-know statement. Quizzical faces have to process this information for a while. This doesn't make sense to their sense of esteem that of course we would all want to be inappropriately groped for free if it weren't for those unfortunate legal barriers. The presence of personal boundaries that coincide with and are as important to the individual as legal barriers never seems to occur to the "business man."

"I would know, and it is not an activity that I engage in."

When I use this tone of voice I should already know that this is someone that I don't want to be talking with—but he upsets me and when I'm upset I tend to give little speeches. I remember some movie I saw a long time ago where the girl (I think it was Wynona Ryder) says to the guy: "I have a little speech that I give male suitors when they want more than I'm prepared to give them . . ." she was then cut off by his response, which was an attempt to grab her while saying something that boiled down to fuck you, who cares, stupid bitch. She gets teary-eyed and says, "You're not worth my little speech," and leaves. They're never worthy of the little speech if you find yourself in the position of having to give it, but I always find myself trying to give it anyway.

I think you will have a better time if, instead of focusing on what you can get away with, or what you can touch or grab, you instead allow me to take control and provide an erotic and sexual experience for you within the limits of what she personally feels comfortable providing, legal mandates, and house rules. A private dance can be a very sensual and intimate experience that can not be distilled into a menu that offers combinations of tangible physical acts for particular prices. Would you rather spend forty dollars to have an experience or sixty dollars to financially coerce someone who doesn't even know you into letting you grab her pussy, at the potential risk of losing her job?

Instead of hearing what Wynona heard, I heard him say, somewhat unbelievably, "Okay, let's go."

But the trouble started immediately. First came the arguments about the price. "No, I was very clear that the dances are forty dollars each, and that if you buy two, you get the third dance for free. So that would be eighty dollars for three songs."

"I thought it would be forty dollars for three songs."

"If that were the case then I would simply be dancing to have money to give to the house. This is the minimum that we dance for if you want a full-contact dance, and don't want to have to keep your hands and arms immobile at your side."

"Well, what do I get to touch. Do I get to touch your pussy?"

Didn't we just go over this upstairs? I have now wasted all this fucking time, and have spent over a song and a half occupying a booth without having swung the curtain back, which is the sign for the floor guy to start charging, who has now walked by twice with raised eyebrows.

"Okay, I'll give you sixty dollars, and you do what you can for that money, but that's all you're going to get." *Great, now I'm going to be stuck here with dickwad for three songs for forty dollars take home (twenty dollars goes to the house). I should just walk out and tell him to fuck himself, but I've already wasted so much time, and with this forty dollars I'll have made my base rent and DJ tip, so everything else will be profit. Sigh. Fuck. Shit. I hate you, you stupid nasty pig.*

I take the money, shove it in my wallet, swing back the heavy black curtain, toss my purse on the table, and prepare to mount Mr. Tie with a mechanical momentum that screams I am not happy to be here. Mr. Tie doesn't notice. Mr. Tie has other things on his mind. He immediately tries to touch.

"I'm sorry, with the money you've given me you have to keep your hands at your sides while I dance for you."

"Are you going to make me come?"

"There's no way for me to know that."

"Well, if you're not going to make me come I want my money back right now."

"The dance has already started, so please just let me do my job, okay?" To actually tell Mr. Tie that I need to do "my job" is a sure sign that he has already trifled away all of the patience that I can afford to spend on him. I do my little dance for him for a few moments until he grabs me with such force that I rear back in surprise from the shock of pain. He takes advantage of my stunned surprise and my new body posture to grab at my pussy.

Normally when this happens I smack the guy, but I am so disgusted by my own participation of having accommodated this asshole with a dance, when every step of the way I should have known to steer clear of him, that I just get up, announce that the dance was over, and return twenty dollars to him. I should just keep all of the money, but I want my interactions with him to come to a close as quickly and as neatly as possible. No such luck. Mr. Tie wants *all* of his money back. Outside of the time spent hustling upstairs which, admittedly, is our time, on *his time* I had to renegotiate a price for a song and a half that had already been clearly set, dance naked on him for close to half a song, and endure not just a breaking of the boundaries that had already been clearly addressed and established, but, in my mind, a physical assault. After apprising him of these facts, I ask him if he really believes that all of this is supposed to be worth nothing. Of course I already know the answer, but I am interested in posing the question because I want to see if he can be made to acknowledge that my time has value. The argument worked to a certain extent, because he starts arguing back in terms of "time."

"We were only in there two seconds," he menacingly lies.

"There are cameras in every booth, and I will be happy to ask one of the managers to show you the videotape of our dance so that you can be certain of the length of time that we actually spent in the booth, and it will also allow me to demonstrate to them how you physically assaulted me."

Mr. Tie is now confused. Mr. Tie didn't know about the cameras. Mr. Tie didn't know that the no-one-who-will-know is potentially the anyone-who-cares-to-watch.

What does our particular "at-ease business man" do when he is unexpectedly thrown for a loop? Mr. Tie, already a stupid, boorish, tedious asshole, transforms right before my very eyes into a base snarling creature with thick matted hair, open sores, long dirty wolf nails, and cruel yellow eyes. In the tatters of Mr. Tie's suit, the monster's eyes gape as if it was unsure of its own surroundings. The monster attempts to reorient itself quickly with unparalleled verbal abuse directed toward me. I am in shock, as anyone who was unfortunate enough to have watched

The Incredible Hulk with Lou Ferrigno can imagine, and also because I make it a habit to keep my conversations with monsters to a minimum. I scream at the floor guy to page a manager, and, finally, although I'm sure only a few seconds have passed, I see a manager clearing the bottom step. I run toward him with the monster hot on my heels.

In the presence of male authority the monster tries to disguise itself by adjusting its tie, which must have been a noose on the now-thick hairy neck, choking off all possibility of air, hence loud indignant accusations and recriminations as well. It was also, I believe, a not-so-subtle gesture to remind me that Mr. Tie could come back at any time if the manager should somehow see the monster, too. *This little bit of trickery enraged me. I'll take a hairy snarling dirty-nailed yellow-eyed beast over that fuck-head Mr. Tie any day. You want-to-be-a-violent-aggressive-intimidating-I-could-rape-you-or-hit-you-or-scare-you piece-of-shit, you're nothing but an "at-ease business man" that I was stupid enough to grace with a moment of humanity. Your hatred of women in the last instance and as a last defense does not scare me, it infuriates me. And, no matter what, I will win.*

The conversation is heated, and ultimately I get emotional, as women often do, or so I'm told, mostly because teary eyes are a sign of emotionality whereas raising one's voice in mock-indignation while slingshotting insults is apparently not. I am careful to pointedly repeat to Mr. Tie in the presence of management that I was physically assaulted, verbally abused, and encourage the incident to be viewed on videotape. Mr. Tie argues that he was tricked, used, deceived, violated, that the manager is a pimp, that this was their game to extort, that now he knows how the game is played, and that all he wants was his money back, that he had given sixty dollars for three dances and hadn't gotten any. The manager explains to him that the third dance is free, and thereby not covered by a fee, so that the sixty dollars was paid for two dances, not three. He then explains that I am not required to let customers touch me, and particularly not for house prices. He further explains that when boundaries are broken the dance stops, and there is no reimbursement for being in a dance that was stopped because the customer has broken the rules.

Finally I go into the dressing room, light a cigarette, and allow myself to cry. Not because he had reduced me to tears, but because I heard myself have to say to a manager that this man is not interested in a dance, or in a woman, he wants a cunt to grab, and then realize the harsh truth that it had been my cunt that Mr. Tie had gotten. I was not about to be a trophy grab for this piece of shit. I could hear them continue to scream throughout my cigarette. The manager comes in to tell me that the customer will not leave, and is, unfortunately, within his rights to stay, and that he will be watched and tossed out if anything else happens. He tells me that Mr. Tie is a woman-hater, that he can see it in his eyes.

I was going to take a fifteen-minute break as the manager suggested, and even went to my locker to change my dress when I thought, *What the fuck am I doing?* He has made me painfully uncomfortable and he *is* going to get the fuck out of here. When I go back upstairs he was screaming to a different manager about the incident and when I walk by he yells, "There she is, there's the girl who violated me." Manager number two is not entertained by this, and tells him he had better leave me alone. He finally calms down and slouches next to his "business man" friend against the back wall, as if he had never left. I approach.

"Do you know that your friend is a misogynistic asshole? Do you know that he threatened me and physically hurt me? Please, as a favor to all women working in San Francisco, do not accompany him to another strip club."

His friend didn't know what to make of what I said, but as I left I overheard him telling Mr. Tie that it was time for them to go.

I circle the upper floor, come back, and see Mr. Tie, momentarily separated from his friend, trying to strike out on his own for a final thrill or two before having to leave. Now, feeling more the hungry lioness with cubs to feed than the misused stripper, I get two inches from his face and tell him, "You are a disgusting pig. Every girl here thinks you're an ugly drunken loser who can't get laid without having to pay. Please continue stumbling around, trying to keep your tiny chest puffed out; it's great entertainment for us."

The manager came up to me a few moments later to let me know that Mr. Tie had left.

5

How You Got Here

Alison Fensterstock

Maybe it started when you needed money. You watch the credit card bills come in through the slot in the front door and you watch the checks come in too and even with your crappy math skills you know that there is more of one than the other.

Or maybe it started when you got thin. You have never been thin. You get on the scale every morning just to watch the needle waver and halt just under 120. You're thin now because you live in a house with these beautiful girls, these special kind of way-ward girls—girls who have rooms full of books and framed degrees hanging on the bathroom wall; girls who watch net-work TV for hours and order crystal meth and cocaine off the Internet and have long, brilliant, snotty conversations and go out to dinner and mix Bloody Marys in the afternoon and sit out on the balcony in slips—and you grow thin together, and sleep too late. So you're thin, and pretty enough, and you listen to the men in the streets, or you catch the looks in their eyes, and you think, somebody owes me something for this. After four years of women's studies you can talk for hours about it but there's no way to verbally quantify the *male gaze*. You just know that something uneven is going on and somebody should pay up.

Or maybe not; maybe it started when you reached the point when you weren't a grown-up yet, but couldn't claim childhood anymore either, and all the money your parents do still send you barely covers the payments on your embarrassingly huge credit card debt, and you have gotten laid off from more jobs than most people used to have in a lifetime, and you can't face any more cover letters and query e-mails and resumes and Web searches and want ads.

Kris, one of the beautiful girls in the house, dances at Temptations. Holly from down the street dances at Sho Bar. But they don't say that unless they know you. What they say is, "I work on Bourbon," or "I work in the Quarter," and everyone knows what they mean. Holly shows you pictures from her portfolio of lithe, gorgeous, topless women in front of rows and rows of mirrors. In the photos they sit with lipstick and cigarettes and loose bills and sit with their backs to their own careless beauty echoing behind them in infinite tunnels made of mirrors and in the mirrors are endless pairs of red and pink lips, streaming smoke, piles of money going on and on forever.

You go out. You go to Temptations. You go to Sho Bar. You go to Rick's Cabaret and Gold Club and Hustler and Scarlett's and Casbah and Big Daddy's, where fishnet-stockinged mannequin legs kick out the second-story window in mechanical glee all night. The girls are so gorgeous with long hair that they flip behind them to splash on their backs, and glittering clear platforms on their shoes that sparkle and catch the light. Their lashes are long and their eyes are smoky. They look like they have a secret. They are special beautiful nighttime animals who strut and grind and glow under the pink and gold and blue lights. Their naked breasts and stomachs look smooth and proud and strong, like they *should* be naked, like nothing is really exposed at all.

Like the working writer you still tell people you are, you procrastinate work with research. You say you're going to work New Year's, and then you say you're going to work Mardi Gras, and then you say you're going to work Jazz Fest, the first weekend of Jazz Fest. Then you say you're going to work the second weekend.

And, surprising yourself, you do. You lie in the claw-foot tub with your safety razor and start with your ankles and work your way up. You stay in the bathroom for hours, preparing. The humidity in the spring New Orleans air makes your body feel greasy with the lotions you've massaged into your shaved skin. You ride your bike down through the Quarter and turn off and park on a corner you hate for its tourists and cheap souvenir shops and bad loud music and flashing lights.

And you lock it up.

First thing the manager does is take you in the back, to a small VIP room on the first floor. "Let me get a look at you," he says. He's gruff, and vaguely Italian, with glasses that accidentally make him look thoughtful, or at least sympathetic. "You have something on under there?" he asks, gesturing toward the tight Capri pants you wore in an attempt to look the part. You strip clumsily down to your pink strawberry-print panties from Target, clothes in an awkward pile on the floor, and look him full in the face. He asks you to turn around, and you do, holding your arms up in a goofy gesture of showmanship that's really an attempt to make your breasts sit higher, your stomach stretch to flatness. "Can you cover that up?" he asks, pointing at your crotch. "Nobody likes to see that kind of shit." You realize he's pointing at the tattoo of a rose high up on your inner thigh. "Oh, yeah," you say. "Yeah, I can cover that up." But nobody ever asks you to again, so you don't bother.

It's a surprise that you know the girl onstage as the manager walks you through the club toward the dressing room. Betty is topless and trying to pull her 1970s disco-spandex jumpsuit off over the anchor of her huge clear Lucite platform shoes. She has tiny coffee-colored breasts with plum nipples and they point right at you as she waves and calls out, "Hey, girl! You're gonna work here, huh? All right!" You were paralyzed when you saw someone you knew at first, but later, you come to realize that there are so many strippers in New Orleans that they all automatically assume that you either used to be a stripper, or are a stripper, or might be a stripper, or are sometimes a stripper, or will be one any day. So when Betty saw you, even though your stomach flipped like Mary Lou Retton, to her it was the same running into you on the street. With all her clothes on.

You are wearing makeup already, and you jump quickly into the approximation of an outfit you pieced together and get ready to hear your name for your first call to the main stage. You were at least ready when the housemom asked you your stage name. You are, and look Jewish, and this is not sexy. You know that much. So you say, "Gina," proudly, feeling like a sixth-grader with a neatly printed worksheet to hand in. Being Italian is definitely sexy. You will be Gina, the plucked and groomed Mafia princess. You will file your acrylic nails, crack your gum, count your money, and pout. But the no-nonsense blonde with eyeliner spidering out into the creases of her crow's feet shakes her head thoughtfully. "Gina . . . no, we've already got Jenny tonight, and Jenna, and Jeannie works nights now. I can't deal with any more of this. You'll miss your stage call and they'll fine you ten bucks and you'll come crying to me. How about Gia? It sounds close, but there's no 'n,' so you'll be able to hear the difference when Josh calls you." She waves up at the DJ booth.

Gia Carangi is the 1970s junkie lesbian model who died of AIDS, contracted from a shared needle. Angelina Jolie played her in an HBO movie. This doesn't seem auspicious. Later you will come to feel affectionate toward men who actually know this.

You don't want to cause trouble, so you say okay. You'll be Gia.

You pick your two songs for your first set. The first is "I Know What Boys Like," by the Waitresses, which you have always admired for its cute, snarky punk appeal, but which is absolutely impossible to dance to. All you can do to the perky beat is prance awkwardly up and down the runway with a nervous smile you can't get rid of. You bought the wrong shoes at the stripper store—Lucite-soled strappy sandals in candy red with no platform and five-inch heels—which force your calves and thighs to stay permanently flexed and your feet into an unnatural arch. You didn't know to buy no-slip stick-on pads for the soles so you mince and slide around the slick hardwood runway in your red-ruffled short-shorts and pink tank top, your breasts flopping around like a jogger's with no bra. The second song is "She Blinded Me With Science," by Thomas Dolby, which is unspeakably worse than the first. You give up and cling to the pole for dear life. Betty slips a pity five in your garter. You pray for the music to end. Your cheeks ache with the ineradicable smile. Somehow you remember you're supposed to take your clothes off, and you toss them awkwardly on the edge of the stage, and return gratefully to the safety of the pole, which you cling to like a six-year-old to her mother on the first day of school.

This is the worst possible naked-in-public dream realized, you think, as you stand onstage for a million years in nothing but a red spandex thong and your miserable shoes, gripping the brass pole for dear life, gyrating weakly with your village-idiot's smile. The nudity is actually a lot less stressful than you feared. The surreality of it pales in comparison to the intensity with which you wonder how the hell you got here, and when do you get to go home.

When you finally get to step gratefully off the stage, you lurk for a few extra seconds in the alcove beside the stage getting back into what passes for your clothes, and are amazed that nobody seems to have noticed the utter misery of your performance. Betty is encouraging, and suffers you following her around like a highly groomed, half-naked puppy. Some of the other girls introduce themselves. Daisy, a freckled, girl-next-door type with long brown hair and a filmy white babydoll nightie, sits with you for a long time drinking longneck Bud Lights and drawing elaborate diagrams of the hotel in Pensacola she's driving to for the weekend. She talks about the huge tropical drinks that are the hotel's signature with enthusiasm and asks if you want to come. More men start to drift in, and other girls, tanned, confident girls who sweep up into the dressing room in ponytails and sweats and emerge in towering shoes and abbreviated outfits and juicy lip gloss. The stage fee increases the later it gets and these are the girls who know they will make enough money to handle this. You think you recognize one of these girls from the gym and sit down next to her at the bar, where she's sipping a glass of the free house champagne. "Hey, you look really familiar," you say in your most casual, beta-female voice. "Do you go to New Orleans Athletic Club?" She stares down her pert, tan nose at you. "No," she says flatly, and turns away, leaving you staring into the glossy waterfall of her platinum hair.

Your stage dancing doesn't get much better because of the shoes, and pain is shooting up your shinbones, but you manage to sell some table dances. You climb up onto a little wooden cube about two and a half feet square, plant your feet and teeter for a song, or two songs, or three. You imagine yourself pitching face first off of your two feet of box and five inches of plastic heel into the nest of plastic Mardi Gras beads on this guy's chest, but you don't. Finally one guy asks you into the VIP, one of the small private rooms furnished with couches and coffee tables and table dance boxes. Once the waitress shuts the door, you sit awkwardly next to him on the couch and try to make small talk. He's young and Southern and drunk and you can't help wondering how he could manage the fee. The half-hour sits on you like lead. He's wearing the frat-boy uniform of white T-shirt, khaki shorts, and hideous Velcro sandals made out of some waterproof futuristic fiber. He is possibly more nervous than you are. This is the first time he's ever done this. Finally you get up and plop yourself down on his lap, and then stop, not sure what to do next. After about five minutes of awkward lap-sitting your time is up and you return gratefully to the floor, and he's out the door and back to Bourbon Street, where his drunk classmates are in all likelihood flashing their own breasts for free or for beads, slipping around in the beer-slicked streets.

After six hours of this and things like it, you dress, pay your house fees, and bike home. Your quadriceps and knees, weak and sore from hours of attempted sexy dips, shriek in protest with every step up the staircase to your room. You will not be able to fully extend your legs or walk right for at least a week. You mumble hello to your roommates and flop on your bed without taking off your makeup. You sleep like a rock for twelve hours and don't go back there for three months.

In the morning and at various intervals all day, the next day, you count up $280 in small bills. You count it again and again. You roll it up, and fold it with creases to lay flat, and organize it by denomination, and face it all the same way, and count it again. You stare at it. You wonder where it came from. You put it away, and take it out, and count it again.

Finally you go back, in the dead of summer, the leanest months on Bourbon Street when the heat bakes the sharp, sour beer and urine smell of the night before into the pavement and the souvenir T-shirts bleach in the sun streaming through the shop windows and the afternoon rain makes steam rise off the street. The tour groups that trickle in this time of year are the ones who want to take advantage of the low off-season rates. From June until September, the thinnest, blondest, tannest girls take off for places like Alaska to work or simply sit back on checking accounts fattened by the high season. So they're reasonably pleased to have you back, even though nobody remembers you and you have to go through the whole hiring process again. So this is when it really starts. You come in three or four days a week all summer long, although you don't break three hundred dollars until November.

And gradually you lose your feeling of displacement and get into the routine. You show up at 9 P.M. every night and leave at 4 A.M., biking home through the dark, empty Quarter, stopping at the twenty-four-hour deli to pick up two imported beers to drink while you take off your makeup and recount your money. Although later you learn that everyone else goes to the bar around the corner at four and takes cabs, all summer you are happily tipsy and asleep before first light.

There is every kind of naked girl imaginable at your work. There are white-trash girls and punk girls and project girls and students and one CPA. Caroline is thirty-six and wears her bleach-blondness and tanning-bed bronze like a tight suit. Jolie is seventeen and actually got legally emancipated from her parents in order to strip that much sooner. Trailer Angel is a honey-blonde metal chick from heaven who looks like Courtney Love, dances to ZZ Top and is nine weeks pregnant. Drunk Angel is twenty-five and says she's been working on Bourbon for ten years, since she ran away. The other Angel is finishing her Ph.D. at Tulane and teaches freshman anthropology during the day. All the Angels are blond. Kiwi brings her own Night Train to work, and sometimes her mother walks the five blocks over from the Iberville projects to stand in the door and ask Kiwi for money. Sometimes she brings Kiwi's kids with her. The money is for crack and Kiwi strides through the club with her wig askew, yelling and cursing at her mother while the men glance around nervously. Kiwi's mother is not allowed in.

Jezebel is a former junkie with baby-white flesh, unnatural red hair, pale eyes, and a huge, pillowy, heart-shaped ass. She glows like a ghost. Sometimes she doesn't work for weeks. One night when you're alone with her in the dressing room she tells you she has HIV and a sugar daddy who pays for her medications, forty-five hundred dollars a month, but she can't get insurance. You spend days on the Internet looking for information on high-risk insurance plans for her, happy for the project, until one day Callie tells you that last year Jezebel had ovarian cancer, and Hodgkin's disease the year before that. And something else the year before that. But then Jezebel stops coming in to work, and nobody knows where she went, and she doesn't come back.

Ginger is a present junkie who spends, she says, one thousand dollars a week on dope and another one thousand dollars a week on facials and saunas and body scrubs and dinner out and new weaves so she doesn't look like a junkie. Ginger also works at Hustler and when they offer her a transfer to California, she starts outpatient rehab, but her parole officer says she can't leave the state until May. Ginger and Bobbie and Sadie and the Angels swap pills all night—round Somas and oblong Xanbars and fat white Vicodin 750s and Percocets and bright blue Adderall and Ritalin and Lortabs and tiny blue Valiums. Callie mixes herbal tinctures and brings them to work in an eyedropper to drip into iced glasses of tap water from the bar gun if you have a headache, or cramps, or think you might be getting a cold. Diamond doesn't talk to anyone but the men. Amber has a three-book contract with the fantasy imprint of a minor New York publisher for a series of soft-porn books about vampires, one of which is already out. You ask her if the vampires have sex with people, or other vampires, or what, and she looks at you like you've got three tits. "Whoever," she says. Kris gets into the Ph.D. program at Rutgers and moves out of the house. You apply to graduate schools, get in, and don't go.

You get ready for work. You stand in the shower, soaped and steamed, and run the razor over almost your entire body. You get out and coat yourself in at least four different lotions, to moisturize the hairless skin, prevent razor burn and ingrown hairs, make you shimmer, and protect your face from the effects of the smoke and alcohol and makeup. You yank eyebrow hair out of your water-softened skin. You blow your hair out straight and tie it up behind your head. You dress and bike to work and undress again, standing in your socks and underwear in front of the mirror, where you apply concealer under your eyes and on your lids, liquid base on your cheeks and nose, powder everywhere, blush on the apples of your cheeks. Then you sweep your whole face again roughly with the large brush to get rid of the excess. You blend pink and gold shadows and dark eyeliner to make your eyes deep-set and large and smoky and shimmery. You paint on liquid eyeliner and draw in the arches of your eyebrows. You dust fine powdery glitter over your eyelids and cheekbones and rub fruit-scented glitter gel over your chest and stomach and butt. You catch the light, and you shine. You dab peach-scented oil on your throat, between your breasts, behind your ears, on your wrists and ankles and the backs of your knees. Then you mist your whole body in a cloud of raspberry body spray, dress, and strap on your shoes. You paint on lipstick last with a brush, for precision; then you gently smear the outline of your lips to look more natural. You pull your garter up to midthigh, shove your clothes and makeup bag into your locker, and check your tiny purse to make sure it has everything: lipstick, cigarettes, lighter, pen (for writing down the phone numbers you will throw away), house keys, and ID. You open the dressing-room door and walk out into the dark.

And then there's your hair. You calculate that you probably spend almost seven hundred dollars this year forcing your corkscrew curls to be straight. You get chemical relaxers at the salon and buy the expensive kind of straightening iron that's not supposed to damage your hair. You buy special salon brands of heat-protectant spray and loose-hold hairspray and straightening shampoos and conditioners and moisturizing shampoos and conditioners and clarifying shampoos and conditioners that strip off all of the crap you pile on your hair to make it straight. You buy four different brands of deep conditioners and two brands of leave-in conditioners and shine spray and shine serum and shine gel. You blow your still-curly hair out into a frizzy mess and work it over section by section with the straightening iron. You get really good at this and soon it takes only twenty minutes, in the dressing room, to get it to look pin-straight and shiny, so you can flip it around your head while you crawl around the stage. You need to do this before you put on your makeup since the heat from the iron makes your face and neck sweat and your hands greasy with product. You actually burn your hands on your own hair if you touch it right after the iron does. You brush broken strands of your fried, dead hair off of your neck and chest with your T-shirt while Ginger smokes and laughs at you. "Poor little white girl, not like the other white girls, huh?" she says. She puts out her cigarette and tosses her flawless weave. "Are there any *boys* out there yet?" she hoots. "I'm fucking *bored,* bitch!" She walks out into the club, laughing at you and your not-like-a-white-girl hair.

You make money. Of course you make money, it's your job, but you really *make* it here. That is, you watch it move from their hand directly into yours, or your garter, or your purse. You watch your income come in physically bill by bill. This is radically different from doing a job and then later getting a check, when, like a child or a puppy being trained, you often feel like you can't quite connect the reward with the action. This is the most immediate way of getting money. Half an hour equals five twenties. One song equals two tens. The roll in your purse grows slowly throughout the night until you take it home secreted in separate wads in your bra, your wallet, your pockets, and your shoes for safety. You stuff piles of singles and fives and tens and twenties and fifties and the occasional hundred in your sock drawer and only take it to the bank when you need to write a check for rent or the phone bill. You are entranced with the physicality of this money. You count it over and over again at home. You touch it constantly. You buy things with cash and count your money and go to the sock drawer instead of the ATM and count your money again and again until the pile dwindles and it's time to go back to work, to get more money.

You start to grow strong and flexible from so much dancing. Lifting your body weight on the pole tightens your chest and shoulder muscles and the endless dipping and squatting turn your quadriceps into rocks. You start to learn the moves. You slide down the mirrored wall, kick your legs together in the air and swing them in circles from the knee. You roll onto your stomach, raise up on all fours, arch and dip your back and wave your legs. You flip onto your side, raise your leg, and hold onto your ankle until your leg is long and strong and white and straight under the light with the pink Lucite heel of your shoe pointing behind your head. Light reflects off of the pink glitter of the straps and sends a shower of pink reflections ricocheting off the mirrors into the club, surrounding you in your own dazzling snowstorm of rosy light. You grab the pole and kick your legs over your head and spread them as you slide down onto your back. You hold the pole in your right hand, step up on the bar with your left leg, hook your right knee around the pole and jump, spinning around so fast the whole club is a blur. You can land on your feet if you want or spin all the way down until the momentum's gone, landing on your knees, so you can lean all the way back until your head touches the hardwood stage. You can climb all the way to the top of the pole, clutch it between your thighs, let go, and hang all the way back, looking at the whole world upside down.

Sometimes it's slow and you lounge across the barstools and drink free house wine or no-name vodka with cranberry juice and lime wedges from the bar. You listen to cheesy Top 40 pop and hang your naked legs over the chair. You mouth the lyrics to a song out of habit, because you've heard it so much in here that you had to like it or go crazy and you look around the bar and see that everyone is singing along and their shiny hair is swaying as they bob their heads and their pink and red and purple lips are moving to the music and you sing out loud and out of tune, like kids on the school bus on a long field trip, and start dancing together in the empty bar. You laugh till your face hurts and your eyeliner runs. You are all hairless and painted and naked and shiny together.

Aaron is the general manager. He's huge, six foot three and over two hundred pounds, with an awful pseudosamurai haircut where a limp top layer of long dark hair hangs over the shaved sides of his head, and an Asiatic moustache and goatee. He's married to the Angel who teaches anthropology at Tulane. He has a master's in biology from UNO and, he says, job offers in research all over the country. He says he's just staying in New Orleans until Angel finishes her Ph.D. One day at the end of the semester he comes home to find that Angel emptied their joint checking account, took the computer and stereo, and left the country, he says, to do fieldwork in Zaire. Within a couple of months, he's moved in with Bobbie and her son. A month or so after that, he fires Sadie when he catches her making out with Bobbie in the dressing room. Aaron has the word "anger" tattooed on his forearm in angry black slashes. All around it are raised scars, some older nubbly ridges, some fresh and pink. Aaron loves it when customers fuck with you so he can start a fight. He doesn't just throw them out like he's supposed to; he pounds them until the street is sticky and red. If you go out with Aaron after work, he sits with you in the bar and tries to piss you off, in the hopes you'll hit him.

Bobbie is pale magic on the pole. She plays long techno songs that go nowhere, echoing beats that never climax or fade, and she climbs and swings and flips and spins, never touching the ground. Her movements are weightless and effortless and disinterested in gravity as she flies around and around the pole long after anyone would think her momentum would be gone. The pole is the center of her universe. She has an almost total disregard for the customers and rarely deigns to speak to them. She has ice-blue almond-shaped eyes with heavy dark lashes set wide in her perfect oval face and rosy cupid's bow lips like a Raphaelite angel. She speaks in a slow alto that makes her sound intelligent and bored. In the blue and silver glow of the stage and the mirrors, she looks like a barely teenage girl as she whirls herself in the air like an angel through the stratosphere, but in the dressing room you see that her small girlish breasts and belly are puckered and deflated with rows and rows of deep stretch marks. On the stage her slight body is white and slim and youthful, and she wears sheer white dresses that her skin glows through in the black light.

Callie sits at the bar with you and talks about Italian horror movies and conspiracy theories and mostly refuses to speak to the men. Caroline busts two knuckles on her right hand on the jaw of a guy who grabs her thigh. A guy from Amsterdam buys a double half-hour with you and Kat, and when you take him in the back he rubs his crotch and demands gratification in his strangely accented but precise English. You start to go get Aaron, but Kat hands you fifty dollars from between her enormous implants and tells you to come back in fifteen minutes.

You get into the rhythm of the hustle and start racking up table dances. Your balance on top of the wobbly wooden cube and shake your straight scented hair over the sweaty shoulders of men on business. You grind your hips inches from their face and don't mind. You're not sure if you mind.

Wait: this is important. You're not sure if you mind. You have no idea. You can't tell.

You start taking cabs home and going to the bar every night with the rest of the dancers. You wake up puffy and irritable every morning and slurp bottled water until it's time to go to work. You start to buy things: shoes and clothes and fifty-dollar dinners out and sheets with an actual thread count and vintage books from eBay and designer knockoff purses and facials and kitschy plates from Pottery Barn. Sometimes all you do in a day is grab some cash from the sock drawer and go out for a walk on sore, unsteady hungover legs to buy something. You lie on the couch watching bad network TV, making deals with yourself that you'll just watch one more show, one more half-hour, and then you'll get on the computer and try to start writing. Then at midnight or eleven-thirty you give up and go rent a movie and promise you'll do it tomorrow. You work less to make up for these lost days and catch up on dwindling writing assignments and with friends who don't work on Bourbon. Sometimes weeks stretch between the days you go in.

You apply to graduate school again, and wait. You meet all kinds of men—men in suits and frat boys in white baseball caps and offshore workers in awkwardly clean dress clothes and European tourists who don't tip. You start looking at strange men in the street, appraisingly, wondering if they go to the clubs. Sometimes they tell you that you are beautiful and perfect and pass you folded bills. Sometimes they ask you to bring a different girl over. They look over the club, like a menu, and point and select. One night a group of four college students on winter break comes in. Three buy dances immediately and move off into the corner, but one stays at the stage, where you are exerting little effort since it's early and they're the only ones in here. He wears round wire-rimmed glasses and is writing on and off in a worn spiral notebook, in between sneaking glances up at you. You are bored. He doesn't tip. Finally you squat down right in front of him on your heels and snap your empty garter at him. "Would you like to make a donation?" you ask as sweetly as you can manage. He looks up at you with all his twenty-one-year-old gravitas and says, "You must be so *bored*." You let his revelation pass and continue, "You can't sit at the stage unless you tip, it's the rules. I'm sorry." He shrugs, unfazed, and says, "I'm really just here hanging out with my friends." Suddenly you hate him with startling intensity. You want to drive all five inches of your spiked plastic heel into his skull. "You need to give me a fucking dollar," you say, "and then go sit away from the fucking stage and wait for your fucking sleazy little friends." Open-mouthed, he digs out a few crumpled bills, places them on the edge of the stage and scoots away to a table near the back, where he whips open his notebook and scrawls away in a frenzy until his friends, drunk and pleased to have been so close to bare breasts, come out of the back and leave. The next day you see the same group through the coffee-shop window near your apartment, carrying plastic go-cups of yellow beer. They look right at you and don't recognize you in your glasses and jeans with your hair frizzy and clipped up on your head. You're standing closer to them in the coffee-shop line than you ever would have gotten to them at work, and the feeling of hate returns until you're so pumped up you don't need coffee. You sit down and stare daggers into their sweaty T-shirted backs until they leave, never having noticed a thing.

You get into graduate school and make plans to leave town. You stop going to work. You stop shaving your legs. You meet Callie at the laundromat and talk about movies and watch your clothes swirl together in a worn mix of thrift-shop prints and denim and scant bright bits of sheer polyester and spandex and glitter. You separate out the thongs from the socks from the jeans from the short-shorts and rhinestoned bikini tops you could never swim in on the table and sort of glance around you to see if anyone is looking at your strange collection of clothes, wondering what they might think. But there's only one guy in there, a neighborhood guy who rode up on a bike in a black T-shirt that smells like a long hot day. He is not the kind of guy who goes to strip clubs. He's transferring a load of what looks like more black T-shirts from the washer to the dryer, and he's not looking at you and Callie at all.

You don't work for weeks and don't want to. You write ad copy and take a research-heavy assignment for a magazine that barely pays, but that you love. You stop buying shoes and dinner and hole up in your apartment on top of the Quarter. The weather grows hotter. You go to yoga every day and cook yourself pasta and make sandwiches. Bourbon Street seems very far away. You're not sure when this happened, but the idea of jumping in the shower at 7 P.M. to prep and pluck and paint seems like almost too much effort to bear, something you watched someone do in a movie once. But you're going away soon, and you think some extra money might be nice. You think, "Why should life be hard?" so off you go again.

You go to a fancier club this time. You sit for hours on the floor in the shiny zoo of girls, too many girls to make real money. You pick up a table dance here and there until you have eighty bucks, but this is bullshit money and nowhere near enough to go home with considering you need to pay a considerable stage fee and tip-out here. You sit and drink house wine and get crankier and crankier until one of the waitresses calls you over to sit with a middle-aged black man in a soft beige collarless shirt that looks expensive. He tells you he'd like to go talk in private for a few minutes and the waitress leads you up to the closed second floor, which surprises you. He rambles on at you for about ten minutes. He tells you he needs to keep it real, he doesn't waste time or money. He's a property developer. He has buildings all over the place. You slouch in the deep cranberry-colored chair across from him and tug at your pink sequined tube top and agree with him. You think it's great that he keeps it real. You think being a property developer is great. You think he is great. You are bored shitless and your candy-red lace tap pants from Victoria's Secret are inching up your ass, but you smile and pat his thigh because he's obviously quite well known here to get this kind of special treatment. Finally the waitress comes back and says, "Come on, Anthony, I need your credit card if you're going to get the VIP. You can't sit up here all night, baby." He hands her his platinum AmEx and she charges it for the half-hour and a fifty-dollar tip for you. She leads you into the VIP room and brings you a round of salty vodka martinis on the rocks, notes the time, and leaves.

So you go through your motions. You turn around, slide off your panties and bend over to show your butt. You shimmy out of your tube top and wiggle. He watches for a while and asks you to sit on his lap and your response comes out by itself: "Oh, we usually get a tip for that." So he places a bill on the coffee table and you sit on his lap. You stand back up and lean over him and dance so close you can breathe on his neck. He starts to unbuckle his belt. You stand up and back away. "Come on, Anthony," you coo. "You know you can't do that." He tells you he's trying to keep it real and lifts his hands in the air to show he's not going any further. "It's digging into my stomach," he says. You decide to let it slide since he's obviously friendly with the club, enough to have waitresses select girls for him and let him hang out on a closed floor. You keep dancing. He undoes the button on his pants. "Anthony!" you say, still in your cutesy voice, and point at his pants. "I'm just trying to keep it real!" he says. He puts another twenty on the coffee table. You give up for now and keep dancing, sit on his lap, climb off, lean back, kick legs in the air, lean back on his chest, and so on. You stand up again and he unzips his fly.

"Anthony, I'm going to get in trouble for this. This is not allowed," you say, trying to make up a new voice that's still flirty but more firm. "A'ight, okay," he mumbles, and rezips. The waitress comes back with a second round of martinis. You gulp down yours gratefully. She doesn't seem to notice the issue of Anthony's pants. He tipped her well. You are on your own.

You are so irritated at this point that you simply turn around and dance with your back to him, grinding your hips while you stare at the wall. After a while, you turn around just for the sake of variety to face him and see that he has undone his pants again and is rubbing himself through his underwear. "Goddamn it, Anthony!" slips out before you can modulate the frustration in your voice. His hand flies off of his crotch. "Hey, it's okay, baby, I'm just trying to keep it real," he says. He throws three more twenties on the table. "Anthony," you say, "you are *not* keeping it real. They have video cameras in here. I'm going to get fired if I let you do that." You know for a fact that while there are video cameras in the VIP, nobody ever watches the monitors, and considering the waitress's behavior earlier, it's dubious whether anyone cares if Anthony strips naked and does the funky chicken on the table, but you've had it. Even though you sat on the floor all night like everyone else waiting for your VIP, this doesn't seem worth it at all. You have handled worse with good humor before, but Anthony is ridiculous and offensive and pitiful and obnoxious all at once and you wish, wish, wish, clicking your five-inch Lucite heels together, that you had stayed home in bed.

Anthony waves his hands at you. "It's okay, baby, it's cool. I know what we can do. How about I stand up and we dance together?" You grudgingly agree, figuring there can't be much time left. He stands up. His pants fall down. He's standing there in his bikini underpants with his pants around his ankles stumbling toward you, trying to slow dance with you to the strains of Nine Inch Nails wafting up from the main stage. "Jesus fucking Christ, Anthony!" you say. You are done. You sit down on the couch and decide that you refuse to speak to Anthony. You don't get to do this for very long because the waitress knocks, then comes in and calls time. "I want another half hour," says Anthony. "All we did was fight, I didn't even get my dance." You stand behind him, facing the waitress, urgently shaking your head and drawing your index finger across your throat. You are a little drunk.

Once Anthony is safely gone, you go to the dressing room, put your clothes on, come downstairs, settle up, and go home. You do not go to the bar. You go straight home and sit cross-legged on the bed with Anthony's money and the rest of it in your hand. You have counted it and sorted it and reorganized it all in a stack. You stare at nothing and think about this place where you are, whether it's a good or a bad place, and how you got here. You rub the thickness of the crisp bills between your fingers and think about going away, and wonder where you'll be when you get back.

6

Whipped Cream, Fire Eating, and the Other Delights of Feature Dancing

Jo Weldon

Some of my fondest memories of stripping involve kneeling on a wooden stage, squirting whipped cream over my breasts. This is not something one generally does in a strip joint; no strip joint requires its house dancers to employ comestibles, and some absolutely forbid it. But for a feature dancer, having a gimmick is as essential as an enthusiastic smile, and covering myself with food was the most reliable gimmick I ever discovered. I probably shouldn't tell you what I did with the cherries.

If you don't know what a feature dancer is, you're not alone. I worked in strip joints for eight years before I ever heard of them. I worked as a house dancer (a member of the in-house staff) in Atlanta during the 1980s, in clubs that were very carefully regulated and completely severed from the rest of the adult entertainment media. Strip clubs didn't play porn movies, for example, or offer actual sex to their customers. Liquor licenses were expensive and were under constant threat from undercover vice squads, so vice was not permitted by the club management. A female police officer was occasionally sent in to ensure that none of us had trimmed our pubic hair too zealously (today, regulations still require an inch of pubic hair in the nude clubs there). We weren't allowed to caress the sides of our breasts, much less rub whipped cream on them. We weren't allowed to bend over, simulate masturbation, hug the customers—the list goes on. What it's actually like now I don't know. I hear that all kinds of vice goes on these days, but that's what you always hear about the clubs you don't work in. Either that, or you hear that all the girls there make one thousand dollars a night. Rumors endlessly circulate in the sex industry.

Commercial strip joints in the 1980s operated very differently from what I had imagined before I began dancing. I had been attracted to stripping partly because of the scene in *Gypsy* in which the strippers sang about having to have a gimmick—I had envisioned myself in elaborate costumes, creating mad choreography, and getting paid to entertain rather than to hustle. Instead I was a drink salesperson in a breakaway bikini, and this was fun in its way but hardly the circus I'd intended to run away with.

One day my friend Dani brought in a copy of *Penthouse* in which she was the centerfold. I was shocked. I had always liked Dani; she was charming, fun to work with, perfectly beautiful without being self-conscious about it, and had a lovely balanced sense of self that focused primarily on her two young daughters. And there she was in a men's magazine, holding her pussy open with her fingers for the entire filthy-minded world to see.

"What did they pay you?" Kristine asked her.

"Twelve hundred dollars," Dani said.

I was even more shocked. Dani made that in a week or two at the club. "What do you get out of it?" I asked.

"I can feature now," she said.

"Feature?"

Dani explained to me that a "feature dancer" traveled around the country and performed shows fifteen to twenty minutes long. The pay, she said, was eighteen hundred dollars to thirty-two hundred dollars per week, minus agents' fees, plus tips and merchandise. "Merchandise?" I asked.

"The magazine," she said. "I buy copies for two dollars apiece and sell them, autographed, for ten or fifteen dollars. I also do Polaroids, where the guy can pose with me and get a Polaroid taken, and he gets to keep the Polaroid, and that's ten dollars a pop."

I asked around and found several other dancers at the club who "featured," but didn't mention it much because of the taboo against posing for pornographic magazines. The women posed for the magazines not for the meager pay (most minor magazines pay only three hundred dollars per shoot), but for "credits"—to obtain a résumé in porn that established the dancer as a kind of underground celebrity. Print porn was seen as more prestigious than films at that time, and there was certainly a hierarchy of the magazines as well. At some clubs, the dancers are announced when they take the stage along with the magazines they have appeared in.

"I'll keep working at this club two weeks a month because I don't want to be away from my daughters all the time," Dani said. "But I really love putting together my shows."

This was the element of featuring that piqued my interest and led to my becoming a feature. Feature dancers, I found out, get to do real shows. They are expected to wear expensive and elaborate costumes, to have worked out at least minimal choreography, and to have "themes" for their shows. One of the most popular, Dani told me, was "Hot for Teacher," in which the dancer started out dressed as a teacher and stripped down to dominatrix gear, and then punished one of the "bad boys" from the audience. "But you can do anything," she said. "I saw one girl act out a scene from the *Wizard of Oz,* and another who didn't have themes but did the most incredible gymnastics."

I also discovered that it is usually the less prestigious clubs who employ feature dancers, probably why I hadn't learned of their existence beforehand. While many managers told me that they loved the air of excitement and glamour that feature dancers added to the environment of the club, it was clear to me that most "upscale" clubs wished to disassociate themselves from the pornography industry.

Dani connected me with an agent, who turned out to be an old friend of mine, Pete Palumbo. "The main thing, once you get your credits, is attitude and reliability," Pete informed me. "You've got to be easy to work with and you've got to be reliable." This made sense to me. All of the feature dancers are centerfold-attractive, many of them phenomenally so; this being a given, it virtually eliminates the element of looks from consideration.

That was right up my alley. I had a work ethic that actually worked against me as a house dancer—I was so reliable and easygoing that some strip-joint managers didn't respect me for not being diva enough. "How do I get credits?" I asked him.

"You need to do *Hustler,* or something. Any magazine will do to get you started out."

Hustler! Ack! I was a big fan of Larry Flynt's lawyers and their anticensorship achievements, but I had an abiding wariness of the magazine, not to mention Flynt himself. "What about

Playboy?" I had issues with *Playboy* too, but I won't get into that, and at the moment, it seemed more palatable than *Hustler*.

Pete kindly did not point out that, at thirty years old and five feet tall, I wasn't the most likely candidate for *Playboy*. He did, however, share some quite practical information: "*Playboy* makes the models sign a contract that states that they can't use the *Playboy* name to promote themselves for five years, so it's useless as a feature promotion."

"Dani uses *Playboy* as one of her credits."

"No, that's *Playboy Lingerie,* not the same thing at all." So much to learn!

Whatever. I wanted to be a feature. I'd do *Hustler,* the least prestigious magazine in the world, if it meant that I could finally do a fan dance like my hero Sally Rand.

Pete took Polaroids of me and sent them out to photographers in New York, Florida, and Los Angeles. The photographers reviewed my Polaroids and I got my first modeling assignment with Suze Randall, who had sent my Polaroids along to *Swank* and had gotten preapproval for the shoot. "Suze might also be able to get you into *Penthouse,*" Pete said. *Penthouse* was the best credit a magazine model could have, because they placed very few restrictions on features, and recent Penthouse Pets could get as much as thirty-five hundred dollars per week. Amber Lynn was getting eighteen thousand dollars per week at the time, but I knew I'd never be a porn star, so I was more than happy with the pay at the lower levels.

Suze bought me a plane ticket and flew me out to LA. This was 1993; current magazine models tell me that photographers are no longer able to get preapproval, and that the best way to get into magazines is to go to LA, stay for a few weeks, and take your own Polaroids to the photographers. At that time, however, my transportation and lodging were covered, and my appearance in the magazine was a sure thing.

I decided to work under the stage name "Tanya Hyde," because I was working the fetish angle (something that didn't always go over in strip clubs as a house dancer yet) and because I love bad puns.

The photo shoot itself was great fun. I had never done porn, but it was easy. Again, this being 1992, I was not expected to penetrate myself, and the market was predominated by straightforward single-girl shoots. The current trend is to have two or more models, preferably a male/female couple, but when I was modeling there was no pressure whatsoever. I just had to spend two hours accumulating a ridiculous amount of makeup on my face, having my pubic hair minimized, and my public hair maximized. Then I was carefully posed on furniture that was rented for the day, and Suze and Emma told me how gorgeous I was for four hours while I held-held-held the difficult positions, all of which had names just like the ballet positions I learned in high school (laying on one's back with one's legs pointing to the side is called "The Dolphin," for example).

While waiting for the magazines to come out, I put my shows together. I had to have a minimum of eight, all flexible for the various county laws I'd be subject to—some counties required G-strings, some full bottoms, and some allowed the dancers to go nude. I had to have tapes of music for my shows made by a professional DJ. I had to get a storage space for the costumes and trunks. In one night, I made a breakaway white satin wedding dress so that I could do the expected, but always appreciated, "White Wedding" dance. At the end of all this preparation I had eight thousand dollars in receipts to deduct from my taxes.

As the dancers tell Natalie Wood in *Gypsy*, you gotta have a gimmick. A feature, however, needs to have as many gimmicks as possible, usually during the last song of her set. I was neither a spectacular dancer nor unusually beautiful for a feature, so I relied on props and food. At the climax of the wedding show, I covered myself in whipped cream—in one year of feature dancing I bought over one hundred cans of the stuff, as this turned out to be by far the most popular of my shows. No matter how many times I did it, the crowd always burst into a gratifying roar of applause at my willingness to make a mess of myself. I didn't stop at whipped cream. At the climax of my hippie act, I let men paint on me with little brushes, nostalgically evoking *Laugh-In*. I also did a classic burlesque number that started with feathered fans and finished with a champagne bath. I suppose none of these acts were innovative, but I had no intention of being original. I wanted to live out my old-fashioned burlesque fantasies.

I learned to eat fire from a circus artist named Philip, which was something I had always wanted to do. It was an incredibly powerful, even spiritual, experience to handle fire. I learned to run the fire wand down my arm so that a trail of blue flame remained for seconds afterward, and though I've now done it hundreds of times, the thrill and the fear have never passed. At that time fetish was not remotely mainstream and I intended to use my background in S/M to set myself apart. I rigged a whip with a bulb of fake blood so that when I swung it across my back, it left bloody stripes. (This went over better than one might think as a feature, although one club manager forbade me to do it because it was, in his words, "too political.")

All the magazines came out at once; suddenly my pussy was everywhere. I was *Cheri* magazine's Tart of the Month, a title that thoroughly amused me; I was in an international issue of

Penthouse (not as prestigious as U.S. *Penthouse*, but good enough); I was in *Swank*, *Live*, *Oui*, and other lower-echelon magazines. *Hustler*, oddly enough, rejected me, which I found ironic—"You mean," I said to Pete, "that I'm willing to lower myself to be in their funky magazine, and they won't have me?" Pete laughed.

I was booked into a club in Long Island, New York, called Mirage. The owners treated me like a star and the other dancers were friendly and enthusiastic, encouraging the customers to tip me and participate in my shows. The counterman at the deli recognized me from my ad in the local paper and gave me free bagels.

In some clubs the dancers were hostile. At one club, I was fired after my first show and left stranded in Miami. (I'm still not sure what actually happened, but I heard that one of my agents lost my promotional materials—expensive to reproduce—and sent photos of another feature dancer instead). But for the most part I was treated very well. One particularly pleasant memory is of my friend Judith coming to a club to keep me company and "roadie" for me. I had one show during which I would cover myself with honey and allow the customers to stick dollar bills to me; Judith helped me literally launder the money.

I worked as a feature for only about a year and a half, but it turns out that I absolutely loathe traveling. I tried featuring just one week a month while keeping two shifts a week at a local club, but that didn't justify the expense of maintaining costumes and keeping a separate storage space for all my gear. In the end I sold most of my costumes to another feature dancer. In those eighteen months, however, I managed to get entirely out of some medical debt I had incurred and to pay off a new car.

In 1994, I was asked to do a weekly column about stripping for a local paper. I used the opportunity to interview other feature dancers who came through town. Like myself, many of the other features I spoke with enjoyed the performance aspect much more than they had enjoyed socializing and getting table dances as house dancers. (To the outsider, it looks as if the customer gets the table dance; to the career stripper, however, "getting" a dance is the literal equivalent of making a sale.) Busty Dusty, a feature whose breasts are bigger than my head, said, "I don't like to sit down and have a meaningless conversation with someone I don't know. I'd rather put a beer bottle in between my boobs and feed it to them without using my hands." Others, like Cheyenne Autumn, valued the experience most for the ability to express their spirituality—and years of formal dance training. Porn star Nina Hartley's favorite part of performing was the question and answer section of her show. I once saw her do this, and when a member of the audience asked her how much she liked "taking it up the ass," she grinned and said, "About as much as you would, honey!"

Others were more creative in an entrepreneurial fashion. Melissa Wolf developed an ingenious approach to self-promotion that led to many of the traditions feature dancers take for granted today—selling posters, T-shirts, and mouse pads with their images on them, just like rock stars. Melissa was able to buy two Baskin-Robbins franchises after ten years of turning herself into a banana split (complete with chocolate syrup and nuts) on strip-joint stages.

One of today's most popular features, Dita Von Teese, has contributed to the popularity of the current burlesque revival with her vintage-styled fan dances and champagne bath shows, the kinds of shows that inspired me in my youth. My lust (it might not be amiss to call it a compulsion) to perform has led me to participate in postmodern burlesque shows in Manhattan.

The shows operate in an underground and distinctly carny fashion, entirely unlike the corporate environment of today's strip joints. I make no money to speak of by doing this, but I'm able to perform as a kind of female drag queen, expressing my mixed feelings about my former profession as a table dancer by satirizing every move I utilized to make money in my heyday. While my sense of irony (few things are more ironic than a stripper's onstage smile) was no more intense then than it is today, the irony itself has become my gimmick and my glamour.

SECTION TWO: Flirtation

7

Why I Go to Strip Clubs

Émile Blauche

A certain Byzantine Bishop had said upon seeing a singer of Antioch, "I looked long upon her beauty, knowing that I would behold it upon the day of judgment, and I wept to remember that I had taken less care of my soul than she of her body."

—Yeats, *A Vision*

Why I go to strip clubs:

Because there are no other places quite like them; because Hollywood movies get them all wrong; because politicians get them all wrong; because moralists get them all wrong; because the mixture of artifice and truth in a strip club can be intoxicating; because most stereotypes about dancers are untrue; because occasionally the DJ plays a song that trances me; because sometimes I just want to go braindead; because my head gets filled with images rather than words; because there might really be a true amateur in the amateur contest this time; because the feature dancers are never as good as the local ones; because I take a perverse pleasure in being reminded why I detest middle-aged, cigar-smoking, overgrown fratboys so much; because I believe that some dancers are really my friends; because I just got a call on my cell from MacKenzie (or Nadia or Cecelia), and she'd be pissed if I didn't show up; because three dimensions beat two; because I'm not convinced you can really tire of the feminine form in its multitudinous splendor; because most dancers look as good in the daylight or in street clothes; because I can look and sometimes I learn I don't even want to; because I discovered once what my ideal female body was and it made me sad to know that I would never hold it but happy to know that someone else would; because my friend Luke calls our favorite lap-dance club "the grind factory," and that seems right; because there's a certain power in refusing the offer of a woman more beautiful than me; because I always leave the club broke or depressed or both; because I'm approached in the clubs; because I can approach; because I know she won't go home with me; because she speaks French in my ear while she dances; because she couldn't possibly know I understand every word; because when she sat down at my table she looked in my eyes and saw sadness; because she was the first person that day to remark on it; because in every city, every region, every country, the clubs are just different enough to be fascinating; because I don't know where else to go in a strange city; because places like New Orleans's Bourbon Street, Baltimore's "Block," and Paris's Pigalle exist; because some of the best people I've met and greatest times I've had have been in a strip club; because once, after being ripped off in a private room upstairs, my friend and I concluded that we are "very small men"; because I want to prove to dancers that not all men are pigs;

because once I talked a dancer out of getting implants; because I can't believe she's really going out with him; because I have been to more clubs than anyone I know; because the first time I went to a club I cried afterward and I wanted to know why; because once I went to the opera and then to a strip club afterward and I liked the juxtaposition; because once I helped a dancer over the death of a close friend; because the waitress already knows what I want to drink; because dancers seem to find other dancers attractive; because sometimes they find me attractive; because I have learned a lot about myself and others; because I like to watch; because there are other people who like to watch, too; because I hate to watch TV; because you can tell a lot about a person from their attitude toward strippers and behavior in a strip club; because she can close her eyes and get lost in her body's movements; because her skin is so smooth; because "her skin makes me cry," as the Radiohead song has it; because she makes me feel weak; because she makes me feel powerful; because I wish I were her for a night; because I have never felt a dancer was beneath me; because a dollar tip doesn't seem appropriate for the amazing things she just did onstage but that's what I want to spend at that moment; because I don't really know what the hell I'm paying for anyway; because spending money in a strip club proves the absurdity of capitalism; because nudity can be absurd; because dancers know that; because I need a reminder that there is beauty in the world; because this place is alive and I fear death; and, most of all, because sometimes when the world is really, really shitty, I close my eyes and see her liquid movements.

8

Becoming a Regular

John Smith

I could hardly breathe. It felt great. Sunny—she used her real name since it sounded fake anyway—sat up and pulled her breasts off my face. I'd wondered why she had taken my glasses off when I decided to try a private dance. I expected the kind of dance I'd gotten in New Orleans, that city of sensuality and danger. The dancer there had sat on a table in front of me, teasing me with her breasts and face and hips. I thought I would get the same show here, but with Sunny sitting on my lap instead of on a table. I didn't know if the smile she gave me was sincere, or if she was trying to conceal a laugh after seeing my startled expression when she told me I didn't have to keep my hands at my side. Or maybe it was the smile emerging on my face that led to hers. I didn't leave with very much money, though I did leave with her perfume on me. I asked her what the scent was. The answer was both telling and prescient. It was Obsession.

In *Swimming to Cambodia,* Spalding Gray describes his search for the "perfect moment." I felt I'd had one, and kept replaying the dance in my mind. In the car driving home, probably going too fast, I turned the CD player way up, and found that every song on the disc needed one more voice, mine, singing along at top volume. By the time I had arrived home an hour later, I was closer to earth. My wife, Karen, asked how my visit was. "Fine," I said. I wanted to say so much more, but that's all she wanted to hear. It isn't like us not to share everything. I wished she'd want to go with me next time and share the fun, but that wouldn't be her.

Sunny had unbuttoned my shirt in the club. When I took off my sweater, I noticed that I had rebuttoned my shirt with the buttons and holes off by one. Karen didn't see.

I was now a regular. The parking valet would say, "Welcome back," and the restroom valet would say, "Hey, boss, good to see you again." Carlos's job was to press the top of the soap dispenser when you washed your hands and to hand you a paper towel to dry them. He was a living Ellis Island, with many nationalities represented in his genes. He always has something to say about the fucking Taliban, the fucking owners of the local sports teams, the fucking politicians, the fucking taxes. He'd had a long week and was ready to fucking go home, even though it was only 9:00. I tried to help, reminding him he had a great place to work. But he wasn't working in the main room; he was working in the restroom, watching as the customers came in to urinate. Or he'd see the dancers run through the hall, carrying their purses with two hundred, five hundred, maybe a thousand dollars. I felt like an idiot. I gave him an extra buck.

Ron did see the girls. He was the bouncer, looking uncomfortable in his tuxedo. His job was to keep an eye on the VIP room, the area where the lap dances took place. He'd protect the girls from customers whose hands wandered too far. Just being watched was intimidating. However, a tip to Ron would interfere with his vision if the dancer was also agreeable. Ron's other duties included warning everyone if the police were about to make their nightly appearance. For a little while, I thought he had a good job. But watching night after night must take the eroticism out of nude bodies and even watching sexual contact. I later heard Ron had offered a dancer five hundred dollars to give him a golden shower. What will he have left for excitement if he gets enough of those?

I tried dances with other girls, but I kept coming back to Sunny. I was comfortable with her, and she wasn't the "dancer type." Too many of the others had implants, wore too much makeup, or seemed too intent on recruiting me for a dance or two or five, and quickly moving on. Conversation was so much more important than anyone who hadn't been to a strip club would realize. I hated to reject the dancers that came by; I'd been rejected enough over the years to know how it feels. So I gave the best excuses I could, and sometimes offered them a drink if they wanted.

Sunny was pretty, smart, warm, and natural looking. She'd had a breast lift after her second child, but the scars were tiny white lines you couldn't see until she showed them to you. This particular night, Sunny was feeling sick. She'd told me she has irritable bowel syndrome, which was plenty detailed for me, but I was glad she was comfortable enough with me to tell me that. No false illusions were being sold here. Her stomach bothered her and she felt she might throw up. She sat by me and put her head on my shoulder. I held her and it felt good. It felt almost fatherly, though, and that was not good. I looked at us in the mirror at the bar and remembered I was old enough to be her father. She didn't say a word, so I just listened to the music. I didn't know many of the songs, as usual. Earlier they played a great ballad. "Elevator music," Sunny had said with a sour expression.

"I want to eat something," she said. She'd been drinking but hadn't bothered to eat that day. She couldn't find anything on the menu to order, so the chef came out to see us. "What do you want, honey?" he said. He said "honey" in a way that wasn't offensive, but rather caring, in the way an older southern woman might address a younger one. She wanted some pasta with chicken. "You're going to take care of it for her?" the chef said. I nodded, and realized the price had just gone up five dollars or so. Sunny left for the dressing room before the meal came out. The plate was delivered to me, and a little while later, another dancer came over. "Sunny isn't feeling well, but she really thanks you. I'll take it back to her." I paid for the dinner and left. I didn't play the CD as loud on the drive home, and I didn't sing along.

At fifty-four, I'd finally grown up enough to realize that sexual attraction is not love. That took most of my life to figure out. Sunny and I always talked easily, but we didn't truly *relate*. I knew exactly why I liked seeing her. I surprised myself that I didn't feel in love with her. But I did find her so very sexy. And until I had dances with her, I'd forgotten how soft and smooth skin can be when you're young.

Like Sunny, Amy was also nearly thirty. I guess I was most comfortable with the "older" women; I was actually less than twice her age. I stopped in for lunch with a colleague, Jeff, on our way to the airport to go to a professional meeting. Amy was the only one who appealed to me that day, and we did a couple quick dances after lunch. When I got to the airport, I saw pale maroon marks around the crotch of my pants. It was a mistake being Amy's first dance of the day, and I didn't know how to remove the makeup she'd left behind. I showed Jeff and we agreed it didn't look good. I tried using my hand to vigorously brush it off. Jeff said that I might be risking arrest if someone behind me couldn't see what I was doing. I retreated to the restroom, and used a damp paper towel. I managed to spread the marks around, and add some obvious wet spots to my trousers. I'll bet Carlos would have had a better idea.

Since Amy worked the day shift, it was a couple months before I saw her again. She remembered me, even to the point of telling me exactly where I had been sitting. Why did she remember me so? Was I particularly nice and engaging? Or did she not have that many customers who were as old as I was? She had an innocence and enthusiasm I loved. She was very pretty, and had long blonde hair. She didn't look or act like she'd been dancing for a decade, nor did she usually drink on the job. She liked to kiss, something that drew me back to her. Like many of the dancers do, she led me by the hand to the VIP area for the lap dances. I liked the handholding, but was it a bit too much like leading an old person across a busy street?

I returned to my seat and watched Amy flirt with another guy. I felt like it was all kind of sad—older guys, some as unattractive as I felt I was, being made over by pretty young women. I was thinking if I were a dancer, I'd avoid the ill-groomed, the badly dressed, the loudmouths, the cocky businessmen, the drunks, the frat boys, the socially inept, the overweight, the unattractive. I might not even earn my tip-out.

I made the mistake of doing a little math. I am twenty-five years older than Amy is. If the situation were reversed somehow in a very different world, my job would be to kiss and touch a woman twenty-five years older than me. That would make my customer seventy-nine. Does Amy feel the way I would feel? Does she go back to the dressing room and tell the other dancers about what an old guy she was just with? Maybe Karen pictures this, too, and that's why she doesn't want to hear about my night out. I decided against another gin and tonic.

Donnie's Dollhouse is not the upscale bar where Sunny usually works. Sunny's husband told me she'd be working there tonight if I wanted to see her. It's close to her home and she's been working there lately so she'll have less time on the road. The cinder-block walls are painted with pictures of girls with impossible figures. There's a pool table inside surrounded by knotty pine walls. The walls are filled with beer posters and the warning, "You must purchase a drink every half hour." The guys mostly wear T-shirts and ball caps, and you'd be self-conscious ordering anything but beer. The dancers generally didn't look as good: they weren't as attractive, had worse teeth, or weren't as articulate. The stage dances were raunchier.

Sunny ran over to me when I came in, hugged me, and told me it was my lucky night—that she was drunk. She has me buy her a drink, and it's gone when I next look at the table. When she's been drinking, she talks nonstop. It's entertaining and the conversation usually has a sexual content. The dances she gives me are no longer just great; they're awesome. She overdoes it a bit, moaning "oh, oh, oh" in an unconvincing way. She reminds me of a woman in a porn film who's moaning and saying, "oh, baby"—but her lips aren't moving, or they are otherwise engaged; the words have clearly been added later. But I don't think she intended for me to take her sounds seriously. We're just having some fun. She jokes that I've been "cheating" on her by seeing Amy.

The private dance area is unsupervised, and I'm having a great time. She says she is, too. She's totally convincing. Yet, unlike me, she always knows exactly how many dances we've done. She tells me I'm really hard that night. Viagra—the drug of choice for the normal fifty-four-year-old who wants to be a normal twenty-four-year-old for a couple hours. I didn't know how relaxed I'd be in this bar, and better not to worry about how I'd respond.

I have wonderful fun with her, yet there's this nagging concern—is the job so tough that she has to drink to get through the night? I know once a manager was worried about her and drove behind her for many miles to make sure she wouldn't be driving erratically. He was going to stop her if she did. What if I buy her the last drink she has before she goes home, and she gets in an accident? I call her the next day to make sure she got back okay. She's taking care of her toddler and her older son, and things sound hectic. I wonder how she manages to be a nearly straight-A student. I apologize for doing more touching last night than I know she's comfortable with. She laughs, says she doesn't remember, but she's glad I feel guilty.

Guilt is not something I experience much, but have had more of since going to the clubs. I try to go when Karen has other things going on, so I'm not taking much time away from her. I wonder if I could sneak away, would I do it? But I'm not a good liar, I like honesty, it's a two-hour round-trip drive, and I usually come back with some degree of smoke smell. I've never smoked a cigarette in my life.

* * *

The guilt is mostly over the money. I'm the type of person who can agonize over a twenty-dollar purchase, consult *Consumer Reports,* and finally wait for a sale. But buying some twenty-dollar dances are nothing, and then there's the tip. A few days before I went to Donnie's, Karen and I made food and gave a cash donation for dinner for the women at the domestic violence shelter. How many more meals could we have given with the money I'd spent on dances in the past year? If I had used my money to make a bigger donation to Planned Parenthood, would there maybe be someone who wouldn't have had a child and taken a dancing job she didn't want?

I have developed a silly and fruitless series of rationalizations. I didn't take a vacation this summer, so I saved money there. Karen spent sixteen hundred dollars on landscaping that was mostly for her, so now it's my turn to spend. I'll teach a summer-school course next summer and make far more than I've been spending. After 9/11, you never know what's going to happen, so you've got to enjoy life. But one previous rationalization has flown out the window—that I'll simply go less often. I'm hooked.

The dances themselves don't make me feel guilty. If anything, I think that they're somehow due me—that it's my time—that this is what other guys experienced during their college years that I did not. A therapist I once met told a story of how his child didn't seem to appreciate the fresh fruit the family had. He told his son, "You should have these strawberries. When I was a boy, we were poor. We sometimes didn't have enough to eat. I loved strawberries, but we couldn't afford them." His son noticed the sadness in his father's eyes. The boy brightened and said, "Well, dad, you can have some now!" The kid was onto something.

* * *

I have a lot of sales resistance. I hate being manipulated. So why do those characteristics disappear when I'm in the club? I know exactly why Amy and Sunny seem so glad to see me. I can watch them with others and see just how they work. I can see them use their tricks on me and I don't care. Instead, I think to myself, *Money can buy happiness.*

I ask Amy if she likes girls—many of the dancers here claim to be bisexual. Amy turns the question around on me: "Do *you* like girls who like girls?" Ah, the answer of someone who has worked the job for a decade. Actually, it was more transparent than I would have expected of her. She should have been able to guess. Yeah, I like girls who like girls. And, amazingly, she likes girls! Yes, she'd *love* to do a private dance with Sunny for me.

What could be better than living out a longtime fantasy? A lot of things, it turns out, including keeping a fantasy just a fantasy. Amy called Sunny over, we found a dark corner of the VIP room, and the music started. There was a blur of hands, nipples, and tongues. It was much like I had played it out in my mind, except that it was not the incredible experience I'd imagined many times; it was merely fun and erotic. If I had been twenty-four, or even thirty-four, I wouldn't have made it past the first dance.

A new girl, Stephanie, comes by and asks if I want a dance. She's pretty and has a great body. She's the age of my younger daughter, I figure. But she has the same name; it doesn't feel right. I say, "Sorry, not tonight."

Sometimes I lose myself in the alcohol and the lights and sounds and touch at the club, and the world is a great place to be. It's not just a perfect moment; it's a perfect hour or two. And I realize the real world is greatly overrated. But sometimes, when I take a step back, I feel old. I feel wistful.

* * *

I'm waiting in the doctor's office, looking over my appointment book. Nine more days until I can go back to the club again. Yesterday when I counted, it was ten more days. Am I obsessed with Sunny and Amy? Or am I obsessed with aging? I'm waiting to get a flu shot, but begin to think that maybe I should get orders for a cholesterol test. Karen has told me she doesn't want me to have a heart attack in a topless club. It would be bad enough at the funeral without her having to explain I'd been with my stripper friends. Perhaps that's also why she tells me "drive carefully" when I go, using the voice of a parent on prom night. I wait to be called and see an elderly man being wheeled into the waiting room. He needs an oxygen tank to breathe. He doesn't make eye contact, but stares at the floor. I picture myself as him. I imagine him seeing the doctor and hearing, "You'll just have to live with it." How has my doctor gotten so much worse over the years? When I was young, he said "Take this, you'll be fine." Now it's "You'll have to live with it." In my mind, I get wheeled home and pushed by the front window to watch the life outside on the street. I realize there is no life inside, in this wheelchair. I remember happier times—times of laughter, times of sexual energy. I look over at the valve on the oxygen tank. I remember a time when I could hardly breathe.

9

Observing the Observers: Reflections on My Regulars

Katherine Frank

One of the most common questions I was asked as a dancer (in addition to "Are you an exhibitionist?" or "How many of you are lesbians?") was: "Do you like the customers?" This was a complicated question for me. As I was simultaneously an anthropologist, studying the customers and conducting multiple interviews with a number of them, I thought frequently about the men who visited the clubs.[28] At work, I usually thought about them as I figured out ways to succeed as a dancer—how to best approach the men in the club (men in groups required different strategies than single men), ways to quickly ascertain a customer's desires (even if he didn't know how to articulate them), strategies to make our interactions believable and enjoyable for him and profitable for me (I was, after all, expected to pay the same tip-outs and taxes at the end of the night as any dancer, and couldn't just sit backstage and scribble in my notebook no matter how badly I wanted to). At home, sitting at my computer with piles of transcriptions stacked on either side of me, I thought about them in different ways, often pondering what brought the men to the clubs in the first place: Who were these men who were so willing to open their wallets to us each night, paying us far more than we would make at our day jobs? What were the customers hoping to find in our young bodies, our attentions, and our complex financial, sexual, and emotional transactions in those dark, smoky rooms?

Did I like them? How could I *not* like the regular who bought me a riding helmet because he knew I loved horses, the man in the tie and casual shorts who liked to drink too many martinis, tip well, and tell fabulous stories on command, the regulars who wanted advice on how to get along better with their wives, the men who complimented us on every part of our bodies and stuffed our garters and purses with money? On the other hand, in addition to the generalizations such a question would require me to make (Isn't that like asking a waiter if he likes people who eat out?), it also raises a number of issues that were salient and confusing for me personally while I was dancing: concerns about lingering inequalities in the U.S. between men and women in both income and opportunities for sexualized entertainment (Where were these men's wives going when they needed their egos stroked? Did they have an extra five hundred a week to spend on the attentions of young boys, if they wanted to?), questions about aging in a society that devalues older women's bodies (Could I really *like* a man who put down his fifty-year-old wife for her saggy breasts or dimply legs, even if he paid me well, knowing that I will probably be in her shoes someday?), anger over the stigma placed on the dancers but not the customers (*What's a girl like you doing here? I'd never let my daughter do this.*).

So my best answer is, I suppose, that I was fascinated by the customers. As fascinated, perhaps, as all those researchers who stumble into dimly lit strip clubs every year with surveys for the dancers to fill out (*Do you like your job? Have you been sexually abused? Do you have a sex life at home? Problems with drugs or alcohol?*) and rationalizations for their partners and colleagues ("It's *research* . . . I'm not turned on or anything."). I'd been there. I wanted to turn the tables this time, though, to interview from a stigmatized position rather than an authoritative one, to study those who were seen as simply acting naturally, as any red-blooded American male with a little extra cash and some time on his hands would do. I wanted to *understand* the customers, as much as I could possibly hope to from the other side of the gender and labor divisions of contemporary American culture.

To begin doing so, I selected five different strip clubs in one city (which I have chosen to call Laurelton)—from upper-tier gentleman's clubs to lower-tier dive bars—and worked in them for over fifteen months as a nude entertainer. Though there are adult entertainment clubs in the United States that offer lap dancing (or "friction" dancing)—a practice that involves varying amounts of contact between the dancer and the patron and can lead to sexual release for the customer, who may even wear a condom underneath his clothes (see Manaster, Egan, this volume), the clubs I worked in all strictly limited contact. Each venue I chose did offer stage performances by the dancers, along with the opportunity for customers to purchase private table dances. Table dances were offered to the customers at their seats, on a raised platform or table or while standing on the ground between the man's knees. These "private" dances involved a more individualized interaction between the dancers and their customers but while a dancer could disrobe completely and place her hands on the customers' shoulders, other forms of bodily contact were prohibited and she was required to keep at least one foot of space between herself and the customer. Customers were not allowed to touch either the dancers or their own genitals. As the dancers circulated amongst the customers to sell table dances, the individualized interactions that took place became an important part of the experience. Dancers could also sit with customers between their sets and their table dances and make conversation.

I also interviewed thirty regular male customers, meeting with each man as many times as possible. Not every man enjoys visiting strip clubs, despite some beliefs to the contrary. Some may prefer another form of adult entertainment (such as purchasing pornography or visiting massage parlors or prostitutes, for example) or prefer their own fantasy life to the options presented in the marketplace. Some visit strip clubs only occasionally, such as for a bachelor party or other special event, or only during a particular period of their lives. Some men only visit with business associates; others only visit alone. Still others are "regulars," men who frequent a club or a number of clubs daily, weekly, or monthly. My research focused on those regular male customers who visit no-contact strip clubs *often enough to consider this a significant personal practice,* returning again and again to such a venue where contact and sexual release are prohibited and for whom voyeurism and conversation were the eroticized practices. This chapter will not be able to do justice to the complexities of motivation and experience that I discovered during a research project that has now spanned seven years, dozens of interviews, and numerous strip clubs, but what I have tried to do here is highlight some of the motivating desires and fantasies that emerged as patterns and that I flesh out in more depth in my ethnography, *G-Strings and Sympathy: Strip Club Regulars and Male Desire* (2002).

Significantly, not one man that I interviewed said that he went to the clubs specifically for *sexual* release, even in the form of masturbation at a later time. This may be because the Laurelton sex industry is quite large and varied, and men who wanted sexual contact or release had many other venues to choose from in the area. Those few men who did enter the Laurelton clubs expecting sexual release were generally from out of the country or were unfamiliar with the different sectors of the sex industry. This does not mean that sexual acts never occurred in the clubs, of course, or that some men did not desire to purchase sexual intimacies from dancers outside of the clubs for one reason or another. This is also not to say that interactions with dancers were not *sexual* in certain respects—some men did describe table dances as "sexual" experiences and found their fantasizing to be exciting and sometimes quite transgressive.

Most men I spoke with, however, especially the regulars, realized that sexual activity was available in other venues of the industry and were explicit about their knowledge of this fact. Regular customers laughed at young, inexperienced, or foreign men who thought that sex was part of the deal being struck between dancers and the customers. Instead, by far the most prevalent (and usually the first given) *spoken* motivation of the interviewees for visiting strip clubs was a desire to "relax." Nearly every man I spoke with gave this response in some form or another: "I go there to relax and have a good time, get my mind off of work. It does all those things"; "It's a business where people can just come in and let their hair down, so to speak, and relax"; "It's definitely more of a relaxing thing than anything." I could quote many others. In fact, I heard this off-hand response so many times, from men that I interviewed and men that I interacted with, that I specifically began to focus on why exactly the men felt that going to a strip club was relaxing. The reasons fell generally into several different categories: a strip club provided an atmosphere different from both work and home, a relative degree of "safety" as well as "excitement," an opportunity for both personal and sexual acceptance from women, and the pleasure of a sexualized encounter without the pressure of physical performance.

SEARCHING FOR ESCAPE FROM WORK AND HOME

Many men discussed strip clubs as a kind of "entertainment." Yet visiting a strip club is quite different from attending a play or going to the cinema: visiting the clubs means that the male customers will be attended to by women who are young, accepting, usually attractive, hopefully friendly, and whose services (in the form of conversation or dancing) can be purchased for an agreed upon price. It is also a kind of entertainment that men overwhelmingly pursue alone, or with other men, and more rarely in mixed sex groups. Further, one will rarely encounter a performer in a strip club catering to heterosexual male customers who is not believed to be female (or, if not, advertised explicitly as such). This may seem obvious or quite basic; it is, however, extremely important to customers seeking a place where, as Jay Bildstein, creator of the famous Scores strip club in New York City, puts it, "a man could be a man."[29] The desire to visit strip clubs is also more than just a desire to passively see women's bodies, even for the most voyeuristic of customers. There are many ways to potentially "see" naked women, after all—peeping, viewing pornography, reading medical texts, or developing intimate relationships with them, for example. These visits, then, must be seen as also a desire to have a particular kind of *experience* rooted in the complex network of relationships between "home," "work," and "away."

Strip clubs provide an environment where men, singularly or in groups, can engage in traditionally "masculine" activities and forms of consumption often frowned upon in other spheres—cigar smoking, drinking, and even being "rowdy," vulgar, or aggressive. Phillip said that in the strip clubs he "sometimes acted like an asshole because I could," a form of release for him. Herb was married to a "very conservative" woman who did not smoke or drink, pleasures that he could thus not indulge in at home. Herb usually came to the club on his way home from work, sometimes with friends from the office and other times alone. Either way, his time in the club was described as "personal" time that was pleasurable because it allowed him to engage in activities that were inappropriate in the other spheres of his life.

Part of the reason that the distinctiveness from work and home was experienced as relaxing was also related to the different kinds of relationships that could be developed with women in the clubs. Despite the fact that the nudity often becomes commonplace ("routine" or "boring") to regular customers, it is still significant that the clubs are a place where many expectations are inverted; for example, women are undressed in a public space and tend to initiate sexualized interactions rather than the men, sometimes quite aggressively (*Want to buy a table dance?*), and sexualized relationships are openly facilitated through economic exchange (rather than the many covert ways that this happens in everyday life). For these customers, everyday relationships with women were often seen as a source of pressure and expectations. Indeed, many men that I spoke with described relations between women and men in general in the U.S. as being "strained," "confused," or "tense." Beck, for example, felt that there was a "chasm" between contemporary men and women in terms of understanding and expectations, and Kenneth referred to the "war between the sexes." Over half of the men that I interviewed specifically said that they found the clubs relaxing because they provided an escape from the rules of conduct and the social games involved in entering into interactions with other women in an unregulated setting. Relationships formed in strip clubs take away many pressures associated with dating: pretenses, specific social niceties, elaborate plans, mutual exchanges of personal information, etc. There is really even no need for romance—romantic props can be used to set a scene or to individualize an interaction, but are not necessary to move the encounter to a sexualized level (involving nudity, erotic conversation, the sharing of fantasies, etc.). At the same time, the encounters were to some extent "predictable." Phillip called his interactions with dancers "relationships of convenience," explaining that he worked so much he could never find the time to meet women outside of the clubs and move through the expected steps of courtship. In the clubs, he knew exactly how to proceed to obtain the kind of encounter that he desired.

Even a simple conversation with a woman in a singles bar or at another location had its own set of rules and expectations that were sometimes experienced by these men as stressful:

> I want to have fun and be relaxed and cut up and laugh and, you know, have a good time. It's a big stress reliever for me. . . . You know, if I just went out to a

> singles bar, say, then I would know that those girls there are looking to have some kind of relationship beyond what's going to go on just at the bar. But if you go to [the club] you're going there and y'all are entertainers . . . (Roger)

> For me the club situation is almost a way to relax from the tension of a sexual relationship with a woman. You leave when you want. You don't have to stay. You don't have to get to know the person. (Jim)

While Ross claimed that he did not enjoy the impersonal aspect of the encounters in the clubs himself, he felt that this was important to many men:

> What do the men get out of it? Actually, the advantage of being able to walk away. No mess, no fuss, no big deal. You can make as much or as little emotional involvement as you want. You can go in there and shop for a piece of meat, quote unquote, so to speak. I mean, you want to see a girl, you can see a girl run around naked. Have her come over, pay her to do a dance or two or three and walk away and not even ask her her name. Total distancing. Boy . . . I hate to even think of being able to think like that but you know, I see a lot of people that way.

Soon after he made the above statement however, he said that he enjoyed the "female presence without pressure" himself.

Interactions with women in the workplace were also often felt to be constraining. Frank pointed out that in the workplace he felt nervous about giving compliments to women for fear that they would accuse him of sexual harassment. Phillip said that club visits "let frustration out": "With all of this sexual harassment stuff going around these days, men need somewhere to go where they can say and act like they want." Roger said that in the clubs, "everybody knows what the rules are." This implies that there are other spaces where the rules are not so transparent, where the men do not understand exactly what is going to get them into trouble. Some men, like Gary, explicitly stated a desire to interact with women who were not "feminist," and who still wanted to interact with men in what he felt were more "traditional" ways. This sentiment was frequently corroborated by other customers that I interacted with in the clubs who said that men had to continually "be on guard" against offending women. Though I was sometimes disheartened by the "antifeminism" I saw expressed in the clubs, I found it significant that these men experienced their visits (and also, in part, justified them) within a framework of confusion and frustration rather than simply one of privilege or domination. The rapid increase in the number of strip clubs across the United States in the mid-1980s, after all, occurred alongside a massive increase of women into the workforce and an upsurge of attention paid to issues of sexual harassment, date rape, and the condemnation of the sex industry. While this is not a case of simple cause and effect, such developments certainly affect the ways that the men's visits to the clubs are spoken about and understood by them.

Many of the men that I spoke with discussed their confusion as to what was expected of them as "men" in relationships with women. Tim thought that men were under a good deal of "strain" because their wives were also working nowadays, bringing in their own income and insisting that they be allowed to take an active part in planning the couple's future. "She's not taking a backseat to decisions about careers and moves, and I think that a lot of men have a hard time dealing with that," he said. Other men complained that they were expected to be strong and assertive, both at home and in their workplaces, but their female partners were at the same time interested in greater communication and emotional expression. Joe summed this up very succinctly:

> My wife expects me to be strong emotionally, physically, and I expect spiritually, too. . . . But emotionally, she wants me to be strong but she doesn't want me to be overbearing. She wants me to cry and be sensitive, to be the leader and the rock . . . I'm confused as hell. I wouldn't say that openly in public but I'm definitely confused about what it is to be a man.

Zachary, Eric, Kenneth, and Jason made nearly identical comments. Strip clubs offered a temporary respite from both changing definitions of masculinity and such requests from women for either instrumental support or for reciprocal emotional communication.

The home, then, was seen as a different sphere with its own set of obligations, commitments, and conflicts. Certainly, the men received a great deal of enjoyment from their families and almost all were adamant that they did not want to change the structure of their private lives. The home, however, among these interviewees and for many other men that I interacted with, was not necessarily a "haven" from the workplace[30] where the men could simply "relax" and be "themselves." Because the interactions in a strip club (through the gendered performances of both parties) speaks to a male self-representation that is not involved with family or work responsibilities and commitments, the club becomes an ideal space for some men to access a fantasy of freedom, independence, and idealized masculinity.

SAFETY AND EXCITEMENT

I met Saul at the Pony Lounge, a dimly lit club with one stage located in one of the two red-light districts in Laurelton. Whereas customers look at the décor, the parking valets, and the food and beverage lists, among other things, to determine if a club is upscale, dancers check out all of these things *as well as* the dressing rooms. The dressing room at the Pony was tiled, not carpeted, and while there were tanning beds they had no bulbs—instead, they were used by dancers who got too drunk to work the floor or kicked out of their apartments for not making rent. The Pony Lounge, by our mutual evaluations, was definitely lower tier, but Saul said he preferred it to the more glitzy clubs in other sections of the city.

Our interaction was pleasant, and after asking a number of questions about me and my research, Saul agreed to an interview a few days later. The morning of the interview, he called at the last minute to change our location—from a chain bagel shop to a Starbucks. When he finally arrived and we settled into our coffee, he admitted that he had been nervous about our meeting. "Who knows?" he said. "I've heard of men being robbed and killed this way." (*At Starbucks?* I was tempted to ask.) He continued, "You never know by looking at somebody . . . I mean, I would never know if you were . . . like, a crack dealer, you know? Or like living day to day? Or somebody that's going to school for your future." As I had provided him with a business card, my home telephone number, my real name, and the name of my university, I was a bit surprised that I could be perceived as so intimidating. "I enjoy dive bars," he continued, "in seedy areas of town. But I still worry about stuff, about crime and getting rolled in the parking lot."

Saul was not unique, and other interviewees expressed similar misgivings. Could I be a prostitute using the researcher line as a ruse to drum up business? (This seemed like a bizarre ruse to me, but I guess you never know nowadays). Did I work for the Mafia? Was I going to try to rob them? And it wasn't just me—the tales I heard about my co-workers and the other customers in the club over time were fascinating, and rarely, in my experience, based in reality. Such supposed brushes with danger, however, were an important part of many men's excursions. Strip clubs, after all, derive some of their appeal from their ability to be both safe and exciting spaces, and when the tension between these boundaries disappears for a man, he may cease to be a regular customer.

Many of the interviewees discussed their experiences in the language of "adventure" in addition to "variety," "travel," "fun," and "escape." Other men described themselves as "hunters" or "explorers." Nick said that strip clubs provided "adventure" and "excitement" to balance out the more mundane "compartments" of his life such as work and home and that such sexualized ventures "make life worth living." When I asked Alex why he went to strip clubs, he answered,

> I like to do bizarre things, you know . . . Wild, crazy stuff. It's like . . . I guess kind of like rock climbing. You know, you've got guys that'll rappel and you've got guys that'll go off the mountain head first . . . you

> know, there was a lot of extreme desperation and a lot of loneliness and sadness there. It's just wild, I guess. I don't know if it would be a very good analogy to just call it, you know, getting on the back of a Harley Davidson, you know . . . with a shotgun in your hand . . . because there's not any rules, you know?

For many customers, especially (but not exclusively) those who preferred the lower-tier clubs, the fact that visits to strip clubs often implied a journey into "bad" areas of town was seen as risky and dangerous but also exciting, a form of erotic slumming. Alex said that strip clubs were appealing because they "had that sinister-type feel," "you know, the whole place is just kind of like dark and there's an underground there." He said that he thought I was "very brave" for conducting interviews with the customers, and also admitted that he had fantasized that by meeting me, the "worst-case scenario" could be that "she drugs me and steals all my money." Significantly, then, while strip clubs were relatively safe, they were also *dangerous enough* to be alluring, a bit "less civilized" than the places these middle-class men would ordinarily enter. The importance of race in structuring such fantasies was also quite important. White customers expressed concerns about visiting the primarily black clubs in Laurelton, for example, because of the "aggressive" nature of black dancers, the "rough crowds," and the more "graphic displays" that were supposedly found there (though few of the men who expressed such hesitations had actually visited the clubs in question). In the end, most men said that they preferred visiting places that were "comfortable" and "safe" as well as marginal.

After all, despite descriptions of strip clubs as places with "no rules" and as "outside the law," and although customers experience and express feelings of freedom, adventure, or excitement during their excursions to strip clubs, they are actually passing over ground that has been tightly regulated to produce this particular kind of experience. The city has delineated where such clubs can be located and (for the most part) what types of interactions can be had inside. Bouncers physically monitor and control the men's behavior inside the clubs. Even a club like the Pony had a security guard in the parking lot and two or three (usually large and tough-looking) floor managers. Other kinds of behaviors are policed by both the dancers and the other customers, such as proper etiquette in regard to watching table dances, tipping procedures, and customer-to-customer interactions. The men also police their own behavior—few bachelors *really* need their hands to be tied behind a chair during a table dance, and even men who claim to be wild with desire or testosterone are usually found sitting docilely in their chairs. Some of the men's talk about "safety," then, can be seen as a result of both restrictive interventions on the part of the law, the club, and the employees' as well as their own expectations and boundaries.

Excursions into the sex industry are not only related to the allure of "bad" or "dangerous" areas of town, or of the individuals who lurk in "dark corners," but also to the adventure of sexual discovery. Sexual experiences (not necessarily heterosexual, of course), coupled with travel away from the safety of home, have often been portrayed as a form of masculinized adventure—one only needs to think of Henry Miller, the adventures of Don Juan and stories about Charles Bukowski or Jack Kerouac. Many of the men that I spoke with agreed with this idea, even though they were not pursuing sexual contact or release. Steven said that "what a guy gets in a men's club, he doesn't get at home anymore":

> My experience was, the first three to six months of every relationship was just outrageous . . . the quest of meeting and building that trust and building that rapport, to the point where you could bond enough to have sex and whether that happened in one night or it took three months, it's all that excitement leading up and then the exploring and getting to know what you like and what I like. . . . So what's happening out there at the men's clubs, as I sit and watch these guys, they're trying to recapture what's not there in their marriage anymore . . . In the back of their minds there's that hope of hopes that maybe I'm gonna ignite another spark again in my life . . .

At the same time as clubs offered adventure in the form of "sexual" discovery, however, many men also explicitly claimed that strip clubs provided safety in relation to marriages or long-term partnerships. For many of my interviewees, "looking" was the final limit with which they felt comfortable. While visiting a prostitute, a massage parlor, or a "jack shack" is certainly relaxing for *some* men, it caused conflicts for these *particular* men. For example, although some of the interviewees admitted to periodically reading *Playboy* or renting pornographic videos, such practices were not as significant or enjoyable to them as their experiences in strip clubs. None of the interviewees admitted to regularly using escort services, prostitutes, or massage parlors; nor did many of the men that I interacted with on a daily basis in the strip clubs. Several of the interviewees discussed past experiences with prostitutes, yet they did so as experiences that were riddled with much more ambiguity, distaste, or guilt than their visits to strip clubs and none considered this a practice they were likely to take up again.

The strip club, then, was relaxing because it provided a safe space in which to be both married (or committed) and sexually aroused (or at least, interacting with other women in a sexualized setting). This may be in part an American phenomenon, related to cultural ideas about marriage, monogamy, and consumption, as the boundaries between different venues appear less rigid in many other countries, with stripping becoming much more blurred with prostitution or with customers alternatively visiting venues that offer sexualized conversation, manual or oral release, or actual sex.[31] Granted, different ideas about the requirement of sexual exclusivity in marriage and intimate relationships exist among individuals within the U.S. However, regardless of any individual's personal views or practices, the predominant representation of commitment is that of lifetime (or increasingly, serial) monogamy, and one must usually position oneself in relation to this representation. Different men draw their lines in different places as to how far they can explore their desire for others without being unfaithful to their wife or partner. On the other hand, fantasies of cheating on one's partner were indeed implicated in some men's visits. Some of the men, for example, claimed to visit more frequently when they were having problems in their marriages or when their wives were not being "pleasing" to them. In certain ways, strip clubs allowed these customers to secretly release aggression that was building in their outside intimate relationships—they could rebel against or potentially hurt their partners in fantasy (sometimes with real consequences if they were caught), without crossing their own moral boundaries—for a price that, though possibly steep, was far less costly than an actual affair.

PERSONAL AND SEXUAL ACCEPTANCE

One of the things that surprised me the most about the customers when I first began working in strip clubs was the emphasis the men placed on conversation and the pleasure they derived from it. Certainly, such a claim could be dismissed as the men's attempt to justify a sometimes inflammatory practice or defray masturbatory guilt (as when men say they read *Playboy* "for the articles"). However, as I was a participant in thousands of these transactions, I feel less comfortable dismissing the importance of this aspect of the experience. The interviewees' claimed that it did not even always matter what was discussed; for some men, just talking to a beautiful woman about *anything* was considered to be a luxury. Dancers offered an opportunity to talk to women with whom these men would not generally be able to interact, for any number of reasons—a lack of attractiveness, age differences, class differences (in either direction), availability, and the women's willingness to interact outside of the clubs, for example.

Sometimes, the conversation was valued because it was a kind of interaction that the men felt they had difficulty finding elsewhere, especially in male-dominated workplaces. For a variety of reasons, these men felt that women provided conversation in ways that were significantly different from men. As Joe said,

> Sometimes I go there just to talk because I feel like I can talk to somebody there without any rules. There's no boundaries. I don't necessarily have to talk about

> sex but I can go there and just talk about anything and sometimes that's kind of nice. You know? It's almost like therapy. You're not there to judge me.

Roger said that his male friends were good to talk to about "sports, women, or work," but that he felt more engaged with women in conversation about other things. Brett said that though "men can open up to women," men "don't know what their emotions are" and have difficulty communicating with each other because their egos are "too big" and "too fragile." Stoic masculinity may be idealized in the workplace, and eventually come to pervade other areas of men's lives, preventing emotional sharing in male friendships. Sociologist Stacey Oliker suggests a possible nonsexual motive for infidelity on the part of men—as men less often develop intimate friendships with other men, sexual affairs with women may be the only route to intimacy that they feel they have.[32] Strip clubs can be seen as offering similar kinds of releases and connections, without the entanglements, obligations, or repercussions of an affair.

Though the men may have valued the conversation, this is not to say that this conversation was always or necessarily based on mutual disclosure or engagement. Customers could still maintain a sense of control over the situation as long as they paid for the dancer's time—how long the conversation would last, what would be discussed, and whether or not the dancer took off her clothes during the interaction. There was certainly an unspoken understanding that if a dancer was not pleasing, she would not be paid. There were also men who attempted to get the dancers to sit with them and talk to them for free, sometimes using fake financial lures or emotional manipulation. Granted, any dancer could walk away from a customer or group if she did not want to engage in a given interaction or found it offensive, yet there was usually someone else willing to take her place, if only for the money.

Some men noted that the interactions they purchased in strip clubs were an ego boost because they provided safe opportunities for close interactions with women without the risk of rejection. Sexuality and sexual conquest, after all, can be experienced as humiliating and stressful for men as well as thrilling. While the desire for an ego boost was almost never the first motivation that men mentioned, it eventually arose in many of the interviews and conversations that I had:

> I guess it is kind of an ego thing too . . . if I haven't been feeling that great about myself and I go in there it doesn't matter if it's real or not but after a while, it gets in your head, in your memory. (Jason)

> You're massaging the man's ego . . . that's what it boils down to. It makes the man feel good about himself. It's an ego massage . . . giving him the drinks he wants, the food he wants, the massage he wants, you know, whatever it takes. (Ross)

> There's no way you're going to go in [the strip club] and get the cold shoulder, that's for sure. It's just absolutely an ego trip because you go in there and if you're a warthog, bald and got a potbelly, some good-looking girl's gonna come up and go, "Hey, do you want me to dance for you?" Seducing women is something all men wish they were better at, you know? And this seems like you're doing it and it's easy! (Roger)

David described his visits to a strip club during a failing marriage as "good for my ego to build me up, to make me feel like I was a man again." Many sex workers joke about really being "therapists" and understanding their jobs to be about boosting a man's ego by convincing him that he is desirable, masculine, and successful. Thus, customers were at times seeking an otherness within themselves, a sense of escape from those aspects of the self that felt oppressive in other spheres—old age, ugliness, or insecurity, a lack of social skills, or intimate failures.

These customers were aware of the fact that, in addition to male bonding, competition between men also often centered on the struggle to gain attention from women outside the clubs. Many welcomed the opportunity to avoid this competition. In strip clubs, Gary said, "the pressure's off. I have to be accepted." Similarly, David said,

> I don't get excited about going to your local bars and you know, just trying to pick up chicks and be the cool suave dude at the bar. I don't like using the lines and I think the competitive nature of that is just sort of silly to me. The girls at the strip joints might be there not only to talk to; they're there because they're working. They have a reason to be there. There's financial considerations pushing that and they'll talk to you whether you're black, you're big, you're fat, you're small, you're forty-six or you're twenty-four.

Customers also sometimes wanted to be accepted as objects of desire. I was constantly asked questions about how it felt to be a dancer, both on the job and in other settings, for instance, and the customers were fascinated with the details of performing. Often the men said things like, "It must be nice to have everybody want you," "How does it feel to be perfect?" "Is it fun to be the one up on the pedestal?" or "I'd trade places with you if I could." The cross-identificatory wishes being expressed in such statements are rooted in complex fantasies of power, exposure, degradation, and idealization.

Although less directly remarked upon than the other motivations, some men were searching for acceptance of their sexual desires. In addition to the customers who enjoyed the everyday conversation about work, current events, their families, or any number of other topics, I also interacted with a number of men who seemed thrilled by the thought of talking about sex with a woman. As such conversations are often inappropriate between strangers in the everyday world (and even sometimes between lovers), the fact that we could "talk dirty" was relaxing and enjoyable to some customers. Male customers also told dancers things that they claimed they had never told their wives or lovers—usually specific fantasies or experiences that they thought the other women in their lives would not appreciate or understand or that had caused extreme reactions in the past. At times, the desires the customers expressed were simply to look at women's bodies and many men told stories about not being allowed to look at their wife or partner when she was undressed. Paul, Gary, and Saul all mentioned that they had been made to feel like "perverts" numerous times because of their "voyeuristic" desires to look at women, both at home and on the streets.

Many of the customers were also very concerned with seeking women's approval and even enjoyment of the sexual practices that they found appealing. Certainly, in some cases, the idea that dancers would be more accepting of their sexual fantasies was based on the men's ideas about the ethical inadequacies of women who would dance nude or otherwise work in the sex industry. Joe, for example, said that dancers were less likely to pass judgment than other women were because of their stigmatized position: "They're not gonna tell you what's right or wrong because here they are, *dancers*!" Gary made several references to dancers as "sluts," the kind of girls that he could "get" when other women rejected him. Other times, however, men who were involved in alternative lifestyles or who had risqué fantasies seemed to genuinely appreciate women who could talk openly about sex and sexual desire. Swingers sometimes visited the clubs, with or without their partners; as did individuals who had slightly different ideas about monogamy and heterosexual relationships than the norm.

THE FANTASY OF THE "PERFECT PENIS"

It is essential to recognize that the dancers are not the only performers in these venues—the customers, sometimes consciously and sometimes not, are also part of the scene, intricately involved in performances of identity, sexuality, and desire that generated meaning and pleasure out of their interactions. Though the regulars, in my experience, rarely took advantage of the onstage performance opportunities that were available for men in the clubs, such as shower dances (where a customer often celebrating a bachelor party or similar occasion, was tied to a chair and given a shower in a special booth), the fact that they engaged in sexualized encounters with the dancers in a public place, and in the presence of a live audience, was certainly significant to the meanings of the experiences. In such encounters, heterosexuality could be comfortably secured, at least temporarily or in fantasy, through a public performance of desire for a woman. Men could observe themselves desiring—literally, in the mirrored walls of the clubs, and figuratively, in the sense of self-reflection and fantasy.

A strip club offers a certain protection from vulnerability that other arenas—including the bedroom at home—may not. In a strip club, a customer can fantasize about a sexual encounter with a woman, yet is not responsible for actually physically performing or providing pleasure to her. He is also prohibited from revealing his naked body to the dancers, which in itself can provide another form of refuge from judgment. Some of the talk about the "relaxing" aspects of strip clubs must certainly be understood in this context, as interconnected with the vulnerabilities of the body as well as the pleasures. Some of the men with whom I interviewed and interacted had experienced difficulties with sexual performance in their intimate relationships, for example. During our second extended interview, Ross explained that his marriage had become "asexual" in recent years because of his inability to get erections due to a disastrous surgical error. Yet he had slept with a number of women before marriage and said, "My work and my sexual identity are the lynchpins of who I am." In strip clubs, Ross could watch and interact with the dancers, express his desire for them verbally, and be witnessed doing so by others. In this way, visits to the clubs allowed him to access the body that he remembered from his youth, a fantasy body that could respond and perform when bidden to, that need not be explained in a new sexual encounter, along with an opportunity to express his "real" identity (or, to put it slightly differently, a self-representation that was already experienced as "real" or original).

Of course, I do not want to strengthen stereotypes about the sexual inadequacies of men who might use the sex industry. There are, after all, many, many men who visit strip clubs whose bodies are agreeable to them and for whom sexual functioning is not an issue at all. Rather, my argument is that part of what strip clubs provide for their customers is the fantasy of the "perfect penis"[33] without the need to prove it either visually or through their sexual performance. The fantasy of the perfect penis, of course, is linked to hegemonic ideologies of an aggressive or uncontrollable male sexuality, the penis as a "power tool."[34] Yet, it has some of its roots in feelings of vulnerability as well. After all, as Leonore Tiefer argued, "sexual competence is part—some would say the central part—of contemporary masculinity," despite the variety of differences in how masculinity is understood and expressed by individual men.[35]

CUSTOMER ANXIETY

While the men expressed a number of different motivations for their visits to strip clubs, they also experienced a degree of ambivalence about these motivations and about their practices, some of which have been alluded to above. Many men were ambivalent toward sexual arousal in the clubs—while *performances* of desire were encouraged in some situations, especially by male friends, actual evidence of desire (an erection, a dependence on a particular dancer, or an inability to control one's spending) was often seen as humiliating. There are many reasons for this—the cultural shame that often arises for individuals around issues of sex, especially around materials and experiences associated with masturbation (even if masturbation does not actually take place); the social stigma that surrounds the sex industry and its users; moral discomfort, depending on one's religious background and one's other relationships with women; and political discomfort—given the prominence of certain strands of feminism and ideas about "political correctness" in popular discourse, as well as one's own beliefs about how relationships should be conducted. Some men find their desire for commercialized sexual experiences or materials to be an unpleasant compulsion.[36] Conflicting conceptions of masculinity also interact with ideas of "clienthood" itself to create anxiety for some male customers. There are times, for example, in which availing oneself of commodified sexual services is seen as a deficit in one's masculinity, i.e., having to "pay for it" is demeaning if other men can (presumably) get the same female attention for free. There is still a forceful stereotype that "sex workers provide sexual relief to society's 'wretched': the old, the unattractive, the unpartnered" instead of to men in a variety of different positions and with varying privileges.[37] Some of the interviewees went out of their way to point out to me that their sex life was positive and enjoyable, possibly anticipating and trying to deflect some of this stigma.

Certainly, there are some men who, on some occasions, talk openly and with pride about their visits to strip clubs, perhaps even in a way calculated to make others around them (especially women) uncomfortable. Some visits, such as bachelor parties, are seen as socially legitimate and even as "normal" male behavior. On the other hand, men who visit too often or who talk about using any sector of the sex industry too openly risk censure, rejection, and ostracization from friends, families, employers, and lovers, especially if they visit alone. Further, while talk about women's bodies is often a means of bonding with other men, such behavior may be laden with conflicting personal emotional meaning. Many men claimed to feel guilty,

10

Wet Confessions: Autoethnography of a Peep Show Customer[39]

Jamie Berger

I understand that sex should be peaceful and good and loving, but what about the things that turn me on and are repellent at the same time?

—Lisa Palac, *The Edge of the Bed*

The men [who frequent peep shows] don't know it, but they are secretly coming to church. They are seeking absolution, acceptance, compassion, kindness, and caring from a willing, friendly woman—if she is pretty, so much the better. They believe themselves to be fundamentally unlovable because of their sexuality. . . . Granting these men acceptance and understanding instead of disgust and ridicule is the single most profound aspect of sex work.

—Nina Hartley, "Bodhisattvas Among Us," *Tricks and Treats: Sex Workers Write About Their Clients*

In the fall of 1997, my friend G. asked me to read my work at a benefit for a San Francisco alternative performance space. G. is a radical queer woman. I am a heterosexual white man. I hemmed and hawed and tried to duck her invitation. I said I was busy, that I hadn't written anything in ages. I even told her I just plain didn't want to do it, but she wasn't buying my excuses. The truth is I was not eager to be the token straight white male in the show. It's not that I'm uncomfortable in the radical queer world (Okay, maybe I'm a little uncomfortable.), I just have absolutely no interest in stepping up in front of that community and proudly representing the patriarchy.

With about a month to go before the event, though, I acquiesced. All too quickly it was the week of the show. My name was on the flier, and I had no idea what I would read. Instead of writing something, I spent much of my time trying to think of a plausible excuse to bail out: Broken limb? Dead relative? Laryngitis? As the date drew near I anxiously sifted through old grad-school poems, pulling out some "nice" ones: about my mother and a snowstorm, about a fondly remembered ex-girlfriend, about a long nighttime drive filled with hopeful thoughts of the future. Hey, leather-clad lesbians like mothers and ex-girlfriends and hopeful thoughts of the future, right? In the back of my mind, though, nudging at me, was a new piece of writing that I had been working on. It was a short story called "Close," and it was the first fiction I'd written that I actually liked; it was also the worst possible piece for this particular show.

"Close" is the journal of a museum guard named Henry, a mulletted, unkempt, oily-faced junior-college dropout in his early forties. Socially inept and utterly isolated, Henry divides his time between home, work, and a Times Square peep-show joint, where he's fallen in love with a curvy Slav whose stage name is

Nadja. The story includes several scenes of Henry participating in the only form of intimacy he knows: masturbating while awkwardly touching Nadja's breasts through the eye-level porthole of the peep-show booth. I imagined I'd have a hard time reading "Close" out loud anywhere—much less to an audience of hard-core dykes—for fear of offending people and revealing way too much personal knowledge about strippers and peep shows, the sort of knowledge that can only be learned firsthand.

I grew up the only child of two academics, a feminist English professor and a moral philosopher. Together we formed a left-of-liberal family unit whose values included strong stances against racism, sexism, homophobia, and social injustice. Though the Berger family values were ethical guidelines, not moralistic strictures, they engendered as much guilt and shame as Catholic doctrine.

My parents made no explicit rules prohibiting drinking, drugs, and swearing. (Well, words that were offensive to various oppressed groups were forbidden. And the word "sucks" was also a no-no, I think because it debased the sucker, as in "cock-sucker," who is by inference a woman or a gay man. But "fuck" was acceptable in moderation—in fact, I'm pretty sure I first heard the word from Mom.) Civil liberties concerns aside, though, both my parents, were certainly against pornography. So, naturally, I found it incredibly enticing. After a brief preadolescent obsession with forbidden toy guns—I traded some prized Matchbox Cars for a couple of heavy, metallic toy pistols—I quickly moved on to the glossy pages of *Playboy* and *Penthouse*. Soon I made the jump to the grittier, nastier *Hustler* and *Club*.

I stole my first *Hustler* from Tom Denton's house one night in eighth grade. Denton was a gentle giant, a star football lineman who effortlessly tossed opponents about without malice. Then the game would end, and he'd become his big harmless stoner self again. The Dentons' liquor cabinet was always fully stocked and free for the raiding. A bong sat out on the rec-room ping-pong table. And, most exciting to me, Tom left porn just lying around in the open. One night I snuck a *Hustler* into the secret zipper pocket of my parka.

I still have the cover of that magazine somewhere, with its picture of a devilish blonde in shiny red leather, head thrown back and to the side, mouth forming an "o." The look in her eyes is not soft-focus come-hither but straight-up lust. The image, a thrilling combination of the combative and the submissive, contradicted everything I'd been taught. This woman was objectified and loving it. She was horny. She didn't want to be tenderly made love to. She wanted—no, she *needed* to be taken, to be fucked, and fucked hard. This was so wrong, so confusing—and so damn *hot*.

The images inside the magazine evoked similar contradictory feelings, exciting and disturbing at once. In my first, furtive jerk-off sessions to the photographs I focused on the soft smoothness of breasts and bellies, legs and asses, averting my gaze from the pink, fleshy, wetness. Learning to like pictures of women's genitalia was like learning to like the taste of booze. The pictures in *Hustler* burned like bourbon. I started with little sips.

I discovered Times Square in its LIVE! NUDE! GIRLS! heyday late one night in my freshman year of college after a punk-rock show at Roseland Ballroom. I was walking through midtown with my jaded New Yorker friends (I was a recent arrival from upstate, still wide-eyed, just beginning to discover big-city splendors) when we passed by the peep shows on Forty-second Street. I was riveted. Of course, there was no way I was going to admit, let alone indulge, my fascination in my friends' company; it would've been uncool on so many levels. But after that night, at least once a week, I took a subway trip downtown and spent several guilty, anxious hours lurking outside peep show after peep show in the late autumn cold, furtively glancing at the windows and wanting badly to go inside, but always chickening out and heading back uptown to my safe college haven. What was I so afraid of? I can't say exactly. That I'd be "sinning"? That I'd get caught? That I'd suddenly be sucked into a vortex of scantily clad women who'd scorn me and lure me into giving them all my work-study money only to disappoint me in the end? Something along those lines.

Finally, one night I had a couple of beers, got up my nerve, and walked into Show World on the corner of Forty-second Street and Eighth Avenue, the least seedy, most legit-looking of the porn-and-peeps emporiums. I remember fluorescent lights and magazines that showed actual penetration on their covers. It had the grotesque allure of a street fight or a car wreck. A flashing, multicolored arrow that read "Live Show" pointed upstairs.

I didn't go upstairs that first day, but I did soon after, to the little peep-show windows like the ones in my story "Close." That first incursion was both unsatisfying and achingly thrilling. I practically sprinted away afterward, repeating to myself, *I'm a pig. I'm a bad, bad person. I will never, ever do that again. I'm a pig. I'm a bad, bad person*—my secular-humanist Hail Mary.

I've been going back to peep shows more or less regularly ever since, for ten years in New York and another twelve in San Francisco. As the panic and shame faded (but of course never entirely disappeared, especially the shame), I slowly learned how to get what I wanted and needed from that world. The kind of peep-show performer I craved was hard to find. She had to be someone I found physically attractive, of course, but more important, she had to look me in the eye and appear to *see* me, to willingly accept my gaze, my confession.

The peep-show scenes in "Close" are meant to show how unhappy Henry is in his isolation, how badly he needs human contact, which he finally finds with a young museum patron. Though he evokes sympathy, Henry remains an objectifying, straight white male who jerks off daily to peep-show strippers. "Close" is the memoir of a man who could easily (if rashly) be labeled a misogynist, but who is meant to be seen as a pariah, a freak, the kind of person for whom porn and strippers serve a clearly ameliorative purpose. Henry's interactions with Nadja lack any of the mortifying ambiguity of his other interactions with women, or people in general. He pays her; she gives him what he needs.

To this day, I have never caught my father checking out a woman. I've always known, somehow, that this isn't from a lack of desire on his part, but rather an abundance of principle: it's something you just don't do. One time an attractive young woman working behind a shop counter was extremely friendly, even flirtatious with my dad (who bears a strong resemblance to Paul Newman), and, after we left the store, he said, "What a *bright* young woman." The message, as I interpreted it, was that a woman had to be intelligent or interesting in some other non-physical way for a man to like her, and only after she'd been well appreciated as a fellow human being could she be—maybe, someday—physically desired. Never objectified, of course, but desired. Though I don't think my father overtly tried to teach me this lesson, I learned it nonetheless.

I never imagined that my dad would ever let himself think, let alone say, *Wow, those are some sexy eyes,* or, heaven forbid, *What a rack on that broad.* Part of me is proud of him and wants to follow his example. Another part likes to believe that he can leer and fantasize with the best of us, or perhaps the worst of us. Most importantly, with me.

Back in my peep-show youth, at New York's seedier venues, the small booth windows were glassless, and patrons were strongly encouraged to reach through and touch the dancers for a small fee. These women didn't actually dance. They sat naked in chairs on the stage, looking preternaturally bored, barely able to muster the energy to mumble, "Tipping, honey?" in accents that ranged from the Bronx to Prague. If you said yes, she'd come over to your window. (The windows of several different booths would all open to the same raised stage.) "Up or down?" she'd ask. It cost more for down. At first I didn't want to touch at all—hell, I didn't even want to touch the booth's doorknob—but the only way to get a stripper (they didn't actually strip either; they were naked from the start) to come over to your window was to tip, and if you wanted to tip but not touch, well, that was considered weird.

At first I found the experience repulsive and dirty—some of the dancers would even wipe themselves with wetnaps after each customer—but I kept going back. It was another acquired taste, and I acquired it. I always went for "up," so the woman would kneel down to my level, where I could hold a breast and, more important, look at her face. If I was lucky, she might look back.

I've never liked fancy strip clubs. I go to peep shows not to relax or talk to women. I can do that elsewhere. I go first and foremost to get off, and that just doesn't happen at expensive "gentlemen's" clubs, at least not without a whole lot more money than I've got to spend. The fancy clubs are all about tips, and I've never had the cash for that, either. Plus, if a man tips at a fancy club, a dancer will dance for him and talk to him even if she's repulsed by him—he's a paying customer, after all—and the inherent artificiality of that transaction is more than my suspension of disbelief can handle.

At contemporary peeps, unlike the Times Square shows of my youth, there's no tipping, and no touching the dancers. And while it's still an undoubtedly commercial interaction, the balance of power is a little more to my liking. I'm a sort of captive in my little cagelike booth: the dancer can choose to come over to my window or not, and once there she's not bound or influenced by money; she can stay and dance for me until I'm done, or she can just walk away. It allows me to feel that, as improbable as this may sound, once in the bluest of blue moons a dancer may actually, conceivably enjoy our wordless interaction. Part of me wants to believe that if I can make even the tiniest connection with a woman in this most wretchedly sexist and commodified environment, I can somehow be forgiven for my eternal objectifying and wanton lust. Eye contact from a stripper can be sexually satisfying, and even spiritually fulfilling, in a way that cannot be duplicated outside that unique controlled space.

On the floor of the peep-show booth: other men's semen, with its eerily clean, bleachy smell; tissues; quarters that men have dropped and weren't about to pick up; condoms, some from couples who have sex in the booths, but also, I think, from men who jerk off into them. (That just seems depressing; why would anyone jerk off into a condom?)

Once, there was a semen-stained twenty-dollar bill down in the muck, and I concocted a story for how it got there: I imagined a khakied yuppie, laughing nervously at the way-too-real-looking women on the other side of the glass. (This is a quarter peep show, after all, not Larry Flynt's posh Hustler Club next door.) He laughs because it's too much to handle otherwise. I pictured him jerking off even though the dancers don't even vaguely resemble Pamela Anderson. (*Dude, I'm here, why the hell not?*) Then after he's done, he realizes he has nothing to clean himself up with, and, again chuckling, he pulls out a bill, which chafes a bit, but does the job well enough that he can stick his dick back in his Dockers. He laughs a third time as he imagines some poor little immigrant who won't be able to resist picking up the gooey twenty: his cum on another man's hands.

This story gives me solace: I'm not nearly so bad as my imagined yuppie, I think, tugging at my own member, looking back up through the thick glass at a fine, round ass, a pair of swaying hips. I'm a very different kind of man, indeed. I'm more like the women I'm jerking off to than I am like him. And then, just as I'm about to let go, I think, *Hey, did I drop that bill?*

In the months leading up to the benefit at which I was to read my work, I had been frequenting San Francisco's famed Lusty Lady club two or three times a week. I had my own "Nadja," a stripper whose stage name was Sassafras. I knew her schedule and planned my visits accordingly. She was small, maybe five-three, with auburn hair down to her shoulders, full breasts, a freckled, catlike face, and smoldering cat eyes that were somehow simultaneously sultry and kind. But it wasn't so much the way she looked that did it for me—peep shows are filled with women I find physically attractive. It was the way she looked *at me* that made her perfect.

As soon as I shut the door and slipped my first quarter into the slot, she would come right over, say a soft, smiling hello, and begin to dance for me. Eventually she would kneel down, to be at my eye level, and just look at me and hold her breasts in her hands and faintly hum. Through the glass, I could never make out what she was humming, just that it wasn't the Jane's Addiction or Prince song playing through the PA. I was never sure if she knew I could hear her, but the humming was just the sweetest, sexiest thing to me. And best of all, she looked at me as if she were actually seeing me, as if she inherently knew and was happy to give me what I needed: acceptance, forgiveness, release. I had found my ideal confessor.

One day I went to the Lusty Lady, and Sass (as I liked to think of her; "Sassafras" didn't remotely do her justice) was dancing at another window. I found myself enjoying watching her dance for another man, without her knowing I was there. It's kind of ridiculous to feel voyeuristic at a peep show, but that's the way it felt, as if I were actually peeping. From time to time I could see the man's face through the window. He was a small, elderly Asian man, and he craned his neck to look up at her, his eyes wide. Then she turned her back to him and faced me, and when I saw her face, I could tell she wasn't humming.

Soon the other man left, and Sass came over with her usual warm, mischievous smile. This time she didn't dance for me at all, just immediately got down on her knees, brought her face right up to the window and started to sway and hum and hum and hum.

The names of radical feminists like Catharine MacKinnon and Andrea Dworkin were familiar to me even as a preteen from eavesdropping on my mom's women's group. Sitting at the top of the stairs in my pajamas, I learned that thousands of years of patriarchy, with its literal and metaphorical sexual slavery, had done women an incalculable injustice. I also learned that men started wars and were the source of violence, greed, hate, murder, rape, and just about everything else that's awful in the world.

The seventies was a hyperbolic time for the women's movement, and while I now know that my mother didn't intend to teach me that men were evil, per se, that was the lesson I absorbed. I came to think of penetration as an inherently violent act. As I grew older, I began to see myself as oppressor-by-default and—though it may seem melodramatic and hyperpolitically correct today—my penis as a weapon of that oppression. Let me tell you, it put a real crimp in my enjoyment of sex (not to mention my performance), but it added immensely to the rush (and, afterward, the shame) of indulging in pornography and strippers.

The day before the dreaded Saturday benefit reading, I had my little passel of sensitive-male poems ready to go, but an unwelcome thought was edging its way into my brain: that I should read "Close," my museum-guard story, instead.

I fought the impulse with all my might, couldn't believe I was even considering it. But I also wanted to read the best work I had, and despite my fears, the story was, in a sense, absolutely appropriate for the sexually radical and politically engaged audience I envisioned. That night I asked my wife whether I should read it.

Digression: yes, I was married during my Lusty Lady period. My wife not only knew about and accepted my visits, but encouraged them and got off on my descriptions of that world and the porn in my collection. Now my ex, she has always identified with men and masculinity. Her father is a strong, silent heart surgeon. Her four brothers are all great athletes, quietly brilliant types who build beautiful, solid things with their hands.

In many ways my ex tried to be—and in many ways succeeded in becoming—the fifth boy in her family.

So I, who never really learned the manly arts of plumbing and carpentry, was married to a woman who was a professional carpenter, painter, and contractor to supplement a markedly less lucrative career as a dancer and choreographer. When we redid our floors, she wouldn't let me handle the big, unwieldy belt sander, nor would she let me touch a paintbrush when she painted our apartment, although she was kind enough (or patronizing enough, you make the call) to let me sand a couple of walls—after which she touched up my work.

She desired, in an ideal lover, someone bigger, stronger, and tougher than she, to make her feel more feminine. I met the physical requirements, barely. My pervy predilections were my most masculine feature, and offset my more wifely qualities, such as making sure she paid her parking tickets and brushed her teeth and made it to doctor appointments and returned phone calls. She painted the walls, but I arranged the furniture and hung the art just so.

When I asked my wife whether I should read "Close" at the benefit, she replied that she didn't see why not. I tried to explain exactly why not, i.e., that they'll fucking hate me, that's why not. She still didn't see it. "It's a great story," she said. "Read it. What's the worst that can happen?"

I reiterated: the worst that can happen is that *they will hate me.*

"And then what?"

"And then what? They'll hate me, that's what, and I don't want to be hated."

"They won't hate you," she replied. But then, she loved me. What did she know?

I asked another friend and got pretty much the same

response. Just letting the friend read the story had been petrifying. Why was I even thinking about reading it in public? I kept saying to myself, *No way,* but I was starting to think, *Yes way. I'm going to read that story, and it will be great. The audience is going to love it, and radical lesbians will begin to understand men in a new way, and their understanding and eventual forgiveness will allow men to grow to better appreciate and respect women, and a movement will rise, misogyny will die, and peace and love will reign supreme on earth.*

Maybe I was getting a little ahead of myself. But clearly I had decided to read "Close" at the show.

That night, I slept horribly, and I awoke agitated and filled with second thoughts.

Once, I was jerking off while watching a dancer who had always pointedly ignored me. She just plain didn't like me. Usually this ruins it for me, but her body was incredible—long and lean and strong, with smooth olive skin, small breasts, and tiny, button nipples. And, sure, her aloofness was sexy, too. For some reason she deigned to dance for me that day, with just the perfect hint of disdain in her eyes.

I must have stopped stroking myself for a moment and put my hand up by the window (I'm left-handed), because she noticed my wedding ring and dryly said, "Why don't you go home and fuck your wife?"

"I will," I replied, more angry than embarrassed. *What's your point?* I wanted to say. *They're two completely different things. I'm not coming here instead of fucking my wife.* But there was no way to have a discussion through the thick Plexiglas about the difference between sex with one's spouse and masturbating while looking at a sex worker. And of course the disgusted dancer would have had no interest in any such conversation.

Rather than leave chastened, I fed the machine more quarters and kept jerking away, almost frantically. As frustrated and angry as I was, I got off, looking at her ass swaying haughtily, almost mockingly, to the beat. It was the only time in my life I can remember coming in anger.

It's the Saturday of the show, and I feel awful, my stomach tied in a knot. In the afternoon I stop by the Lusty Lady, hoping to relieve my anxiety over reading a story about jerking off to strippers by jerking off to strippers. Sass isn't here, and I'm not turned on by any of the other women, so I go into a video booth and watch porn, jumping from channel to channel: women's bodies, a mouth on a cock, cum spurting onto artificially enhanced breasts. I have to pull hard and fast to get there, but eventually I have a weak, twitchy orgasm. My anxiety is lessened somewhat, but also compounded by guilt and shame.

I go home and shower, put on a pair of old cords and my favorite vintage button-down shirt—a simple, nonconfrontational outfit—and head over to the theater with both "Close" and the "nice" poems under my arm, just in case.

A big crowd is already filling all the chairs and spilling out almost into the hallway. The audience is more mixed than I'd expected: maybe 65 percent women, maybe 30 percent of them with some degree of leather, chains, piercings, or elaborate tattooing. And then there are my friends and neighbors, my little support group. Most of them have no idea what I'll be reading either, and I worry about their reaction, too. I say hi to G., who tells me I'm scheduled to read at the end of the first half. I'll be great, she says. (Oh, how I hate when people say that.) She tells me to relax and gives me a big hug, and I just want to melt into her embrace and disappear. I haven't told her what I'm reading, and I begin to imagine her fury and embarrassment when she hears it, perhaps even my ritual hanging-in-effigy to close out the evening.

The readers who go on before me include a very young, beautiful, gay Asian man and a lesbian poet who is not only leather-clad and angry, but palsied and in a wheelchair to boot. The boisterous crowd is loudly supportive of both of them. And then G. introduces me.

As I step onstage, the audience gives me what I hear as a decidedly lukewarm welcome. I feel big and male and straight and ungainly. The blood begins its mad rush to my face, as if I need to be red to be seen. I arrange my papers on the music stand, adjust the mike, look around the room, mumble a hello, give a spastic laugh, and take a deep breath.

"This is a short story called 'Close,' " I say. My amplified voice sounds very loud. "It's . . ." I stifle the urge to explain or apologize up front. "It's the journal of a museum guard named Henry."

I take a deep breath and look around the room, searching for friendly faces. Then, just as I'm about to look down again, I see her. Unfathomably, in the back left corner of the room, leaning against the wall, is none other than . . . Sass. I look down, blink twice in what feels like slow motion, and think, *Hey, I just imagined I saw Sassafras in the audience. How wacky is that?* I look up again. She's still there. I did not imagine it. She can't possibly be here, and yet there she is, looking right at me—I mean, of course she's looking right at me. Where else would she be looking?

Her presence is actually not all that improbable. San Francisco is like a small town within its artistic communities. In fact, I know several women—one a writer, one a dancer, one a budding academic—who have done stints at the Lusty Lady. The Lusty Lady has always been an offbeat, radicalized strip club (it's the first of its kind to be worker-owned) and, accordingly, it attracts intellectual, artsy employees, including women who just want to try stripping to see what it's like.

So to run into a stripper in my life outside the Lusty Lady is not so unlikely. But to see Sass in the audience when I'm about to read "Close" for the first time is no less than breathtaking. She is my perfect erotic dancer, my dream—and nightmare—audience member. As much as I've always wanted to be seen by strippers, I never imagined this. Here she is a real person, wearing clothes, perhaps even a writer like me. But also not so much like me at all, more like the women in front of whom I'm so petrified to read my story.

For a moment I hold my breath and ride that fine masochistic edge between exquisite pleasure and almost unbearable discomfort. I begin to wonder if there's enough blood in my legs to hold me up. I am petrified, thrilled, nauseated. I think to myself, *Don't lock your knees.* I remember marching in a Columbus Day Parade as a kid, standing and waiting for hours in a hot woolen uniform, and being told: *Don't lock your knees. That's when you pass out*. So I bend my knees a little, look down at my pages, and begin to read:

> April. The weather is getting warmer. The other day I was walking home after my stop off, and I looked through the window of the old office building on West Fifty-second they've gutted and are turning into a Sure-Guard Storage. They finally installed the shiny corrugated lockers. I looked through the window and just happened to be right in front of number 1354,

> which is also the last four digits of my Social Security number. This may mean something. Or not. Sometimes these coincidences mean things.

I look up from time to time at the listening faces. I don't look toward the back left corner. A page or so in, I pause, take a sip of water, slip out of Henry's edgy persona, and smile as if to say, *Hey, everybody, don't forget: that's Henry; I'm Jamie.* I think of the clichéd advice offered to nervous public speakers—imagine the audience naked—and I almost laugh out loud. I'm feeling more naked than I imagine Sass has ever felt in front of me.

About two pages in I get to the tough stuff: "After work, I stop at Babeland." I feel as if I'm about to freeze up—or throw up—but I manage to keep reading:

> Today Nadja is there. I feed the machine an extra bill and give her five bucks through the window even though it only costs three to touch. I tell her "high" and she kneels down so I can reach her. I hold one breast gently with my left hand and jerk off with my right. I like how heavy it is. The breast. I like that she kneels so we're at eye level. I like to feel the weight, the warmth. . . . Sometimes she holds my face in her hands and calls me "baby." I know it's an act but still it feels good. "Baby," she says, "my sweet baby." I always forget to bring tissues.

The audience laughs at the "tissues" line, and I'm starting to feel a rush. I'm becoming Henry, slipping deeper inside his clipped, anxious voice. The final pages go by with a kind of rich, elastic slowness that I've never experienced before, onstage or off.

At the end of "Close," Henry accomplishes something monumental for him: he spends an afternoon with a woman without a Plexiglas wall between them. I feel as if I've broken down some barriers of my own as I read his story: I've done something difficult and monumental for me, and done it as clearly and honestly as I can. I notice my pulse slowing, my sweat cooling me. The story ends, and I say thank-you.

There's a pause, then a roar as the audience begins to whoop and whistle and clap. My applause probably isn't any longer or louder than any other reader's, but to me it feels like absolute thunder. I say thank-you again and step offstage.

G. announces the intermission, and several people, among them a couple of the women I was so afraid of offending, come up to tell me how much they liked the story. A tough and talented writer tells me she's "heard a lot of crap on that subject" but that my piece was "really pretty okay," which I'm later told is high praise coming from her. And G. gives me another hug and, with a proud grin, tells me I did a great job.

Suddenly I remember that back left corner. I wheel around and look for Sass, but she's not there. I scan the room like Rocky, punch-drunk and reeling, searching for Adrian after the big fight. And then, over by the door, I spot a familiar face, and the woman I know only as Sassafras gives me that sweet, sly smile, turns, and is gone.

SECTION THREE: Reformulations

11

Stripper Bashing: An Autovideography of Violence Against Strippers

Merri Lisa Johnson

Crossing town from my apartment on the west side of Binghamton, I fixate on red lights—cars braking in front of me, traffic lights, liquor store signs—sensing something sinister in their neon warnings. Frequent stop lights force me into still moments where I hold my breath and try not to fall into self-reflection. Instead, I check my lipstick, bright red in the rearview mirror, brush a stray flake of glitter from my face, stare at the skyline and search for something pretty in the bare mountains or gold mosque gleaming over a pale brick Price Chopper. I called ahead to say I was running late because of a work-related injury: I got glitter in my eye. This stripper joke comes back to me now as a comment on expected narratives of violence and degradation in sex workers' lives. The work of exotic dance did not bring me the death and destruction promised by virtually every media representation of strippers. The emotional tension it produced was a more refined and banal sort, the same conflicted anxieties that come with any experience defined by competing needs and desires, like going home to visit family, where the different parts of myself collide or are flattened into artificial one-dimensionality.

Working as a stripper isn't always fun and it isn't always safe, but this danger is not inherent in sex work; it is the product of a problematic set of beliefs about sex work and sex workers.[40] The ideology of sexual repression, in its manifestations as Christian guilt, psychological sublimation, or the deferred gratification of the capitalist work ethic, underlies the pervasive threat of violence against sex workers. All the discomfort people have with public sexualness, with their own sexual needs, and with female sexuality in particular gets displaced on to the sex-worker body. We may imagine that selling sex is the worst form of exploitation, that a person loses something irrevocably in the process, that we are selling "the ultimate merchandise," as the narrator calls it in *Ruby in Paradise*, a film in which stripping represents hitting rock bottom. Ruby (Ashley Judd), a young woman barely out of her teens, considers a shift at Fans and Tails when she is flat broke, but ultimately decides against it, making the hard but moral choice, as the audience is meant to understand. This measure of morality is based on a view of sex as uniquely intimate and of sex work as "a fundamental sale of *self*."[41] Wendy Chapkis rejects this assumption, reviewing the work of Karl Marx on the alienation of all labor under capitalism, as well as that of Arlie Hochschild on the emotional labor of flight attendants. Chapkis proposes that the hysterical perception of sex work as an extreme form of abuse stems from an artificial connection between sexual practice and the deep essence of one's identity:

> The respect given to emotional labor
> psychotherapist's office, or a day-car
> extends to the brothel. Just as day-care
> chotherapists who sell nurturing and
> still be able to summon similar feelings
> outside of the workplace, Hochschild ggests that flight attendants who put on a smile along with the uniform are still able to express genuine delight off the job. In the same way, sex workers who sell sexual services may be fully capable of accessing these feelings for noninstrumental ends. The common assumption that this is otherwise is partly due to the special status assigned sexual feeling, especially in women's lives.[42]

Deeming sexuality "special" may connote romance, fantasy, and fairy tale, but it operates in real women's lives to limit how we may deploy our sexual bodies, inscribing our sexual bodies as the locus of possible loss, something to defend and disguise. In contrast, sex radical feminism proposes an economy of plenty—we do not "use up" our sexuality by displaying it at the strip club. We do not render it cheap. We do not trade our self-respect for a sweaty dollar. There is always more where that came from.

Many of the essays in this collection address concrete policies in particular clubs—the hassles of tip-outs, managerial arrogance, and local ordinances. Here, I want to shift to the less concrete, yet no less immediately relevant, realm of the cultural imaginary. How people think about strippers and how strippers are represented in film and television constitute significant elements of the stripper's work environment. The dangers and stigmas attached to exotic dance in our fantasies and films function to limit stripper play, putting a damper on wild abandon and

...tly conflicting with many women's experience of stripping ...s adventure or dare.

WE DARE TO BARE

In that adventure has historically been gendered male, stripping can feel like a masculine transgression for women, a conscious break with the social contract of self-discipline or repressive caution. When I crawled across the stage inside Trent Reznor's scream—"I want to fuck you like an animal"—I was both the object of these Nine Inch Nails lyrics and the subject, the "I" and the "want" and the "fuck" and the "animal." Every word of "Closer" exploded inside my rocking pelvis, broke like potent capsules in my bloodstream. The myth of romantic fantasy beaded up on my face, poured out of me in sweat and fierceness. "You let me violate you," I mouthed to the audience, lamenting the sex I had with my ex-husband whenever he was between girlfriends, and simultaneously channeling that pain into my own active, eroticized threat to the men peering up from stageside with their dollar bills in the air. "You let me penetrate you," I offered, wrapping the back of my knee around the pole and swinging slowly around it, spiraling down through the kinds of penetration in my mind—physical, emotional, intellectual—and blurring the gender of entering and being entered. In the mid-1990s, you could hardly go into a strip club without being assaulted by the words to this song. So many dancers requested it, we eventually groaned as the first deep beats shook the room periodically throughout each shift, but its shrieking insistence on getting closer to one's carnal voraciousness vibrated at the center of my own desire to dance naked, a blur of red lips and tangled hair taking the world up on its dare.

The figure of the stripper in the American cultural imaginary is a site of ideological struggle over the meaning of sexuality, and the persistent threat of violence against her could be construed as an effort to contain what might otherwise constitute a nonnormative sexuality. Indeed "stripper sexuality" could be considered as something akin to other nonnormative sexual preferences or orientations such as homosexual, bisexual, or polyamorous. Strippers develop a heightened sensuality, despite repressive contexts, modeling a kind of sexual identity I long to import into my everyday life. When I lived among male and female strippers, I relished the open eroticism of the most mundane moments. Everything was sexy—our trip to McDonalds to get brunch for everyone, our shared packs of cigarettes, our after-hours hot-tubbing—everything unfolded against the enchanting backdrop of an Enigma disk (it does not surprise me to see that their "greatest hits" compilation is titled, *Love Sensuality Devotion,* as these were precisely the qualities our stripper community cultivated within itself). Having been raised among polite southern girls who changed into their pajamas separately in the bathroom at sleepovers, this new normalcy of walking around in panties and tube tops in mixed company—no bra, no self-consciousness—felt free like France or Mars.[43] Going to the Huddle House late at night in dark lipstick and a spaghetti tank seemed sensuous and urbane. "Yes, we are more comfortable with our bodies and sexuality than most people," writes feminist stripper Peggy Morgan. "Taking our clothes off in public, we realize there is nothing sacred or secret about our bodies. We don't have 'private parts,' dismembered from the rest; they are parts of the whole."[44] In this subculture, being sexy was unhooked from judgment, danger, and expectation. Our visible nipples bore no burden of meaningfulness.

FANTASY

Among my stripper friends, sex was often a mode of play, as it is in some polyamorous communities, not a source of shame, jealousy, or possessiveness. We spent whole weekends on Ecstasy, touching each other's arms and stomachs, watching each other fuck. Sex felt simple beyond the cultural script of emotional obligation or proper feminine restraint, very different from sex in high school and college. Having sex with several Sigma Nus while I was an undergraduate led to the problem of losing my reputation. One brother had the nerve to tell me I needed to "put a lid on it" during a friendly game of quarters. He meant well, offering words of advice to someone with "obviously" low self-esteem, but I rejected the link between promiscuity and self-esteem problems. Free love doesn't always follow from a lack of self-respect; there is something sex-hating in such an equation. In the context of an American culture defined by its intensely contradictory responses to sex—the lasciviousness and puritanism—as well as in the context of my own personal life which was, when I first entered the profession at age twenty-one, defined by an unexpected divorce that had thrown my moral framework painfully into question, this stripper sexuality offered a welcome alternative to marriage and the church teachings that had left me angry and freaked out about sex. Other options were, I'm sure, available—tantric sex, swinging, etc.—but stripping was the venue through which I realized the possibilities of a freer sense of sexuality.

The mixed feelings many strippers have about stripping may be partially explained by this incongruity between what stripping gives us and the cultural perspective on stripping as a job that takes something away from us. We might argue, in contrast, that it is mainstream culture that takes something—our sexual freedom—away from us, and stripping can, in some cases, give it back. In Pat Califia's introduction to an anthology of forbidden fantasies, a contrast is drawn between the American cultural hysteria over sexual abuse, defined as incest, pedophilia, rape, and other egregious acts of sexual aggression, versus a different kind of sexual abuse, defined as sexual panic and the withholding of information about sexuality.[45] As part of the sex radical segment of feminism, Califia, along with Amber Hollibaugh, Carol Queen, and other feminist sexual educators, redefines abuse to reveal how it is endemic to American cultural constructions of sexuality in its common prohibitions on speech, knowledge, and experimentation. From this point of view, it is possible to invert the usual hierarchy of strip clubs and mainstream American institutions of sexuality like family, church, and marriage. Whereas sociologists and psychologists have historically approached the stripper as an abuse victim, perpetuating her abuse by working in the sex industry, one could make an equally valid argument that nonstrippers—those who are uncomfortable with public nudity, those who confuse a lack of modesty with a lack of self-respect, those who perceive explicit sexual talk as inappropriate outside the bedroom or the monogamous couple—are also abuse victims, learning these psychological and social cues within a strict sexual economy that prohibits the free play of pleasure.

The categories of "stripper sexuality" and "nonstripper sexuality" can be interpreted with flexibility, so that people who do not work as strippers may still fall into the category I am creating by virtue of their comfort with public nudity and playful sexuality, while some strippers I have known probably fall more neatly in the nonstripper sexuality category, as they expressed conservative moral views of stripping and sexuality in our dressing-room conversations. I use the marker, "stripper," here to indicate the connection in my own mind between the figure of a woman standing with confidence in front of a crowd, wearing nothing but a G-string and red feather boa, and the possibility of a world defined by wider and wilder sexual choices, where we might all dare to bare. "Stripper" functions here like "queer" does in the work of Michael Warner, to denote a bending of norms, a repudiation of normalcy. In *The Trouble with Normal*, Warner uses "queer" "in a deliberately capacious way . . . in order to suggest how many ways people can find themselves at odds with straight culture."[46] I'd like to use "stripper" in an equally capacious way, aligning this identity with other sex radicals—queers, sex workers, marriage resisters—all those who, in Warner's words, have "insisted that much of what was taken to be morality, respectability, or decorum was, in practice, a way of regulating sexual pleasures and relations."[47]

The abusiveness of a sexual script that encourages us to repress what Naomi Wolf calls our "inner slut" cannot be compartmentalized as the product of the sex industry. It is all around us, perhaps even worse in nonstrip-club spaces. When I check the neckline of my blouse or blot my red lipstick before going to work, when my hips begin to ache from keeping my legs crossed for eight hours under my desk, I am living out a sexual script that prohibits the erotic in everyday life. It can be seen in the "tight and constricted posture" of conventional femininity, to borrow the language of Sandra Lee Bartky's critique of patriarchal bodily disciplines, an unconscious physical "expression of [the] need to ward off real or symbolic sexual attack."[48] In the strip club, there is no such thing as too much lipstick, and it is worth noting that my joints don't hurt as much from spreading my legs as they do from crossing them.

DEFAMATIONS OF STRIPPER CHARACTER

Leora Tanenbaum writes about "slut bashing" primarily as verbal abuse in high school and elementary school, a method of marking outsider femininities. Jennifer Baumgardner and Amy Richards list "slut bashing" as one of the main fronts on which third wave feminism needs to fight sexism in the new millenium. When a girl calls another girl a slut, she is hurling backlash rhetoric that hurts her as much as it does the target, even as she accrues cultural capital by deploying it. The antipathy women demonstrate toward strippers may be an adult form of slut bashing, safely segregating themselves from the pollution and lack of self-respect attached to the sex worker. This verbal harassment—or stripper bashing—pervades contemporary media culture.

FIVE EXAMPLES OF STRIPPER BASHING IN THE MEDIA:

1. On the television drama, *Party of Five*, Charlie has a girlfriend who works as a stripper, and when the actress who plays her goes on the *Rosie O'Donnell Show*, Rosie describes her character as a "tramp," without explaining the connection in her mind between stripper and tramp. The series itself focuses on Charlie's embarassment and on the irreconcilability of being someone's girlfriend and working as a stripper.

2. Dr. Phil interviews a woman and her stripper daughter on his afternoon talk show, and in his trademark gesture of "getting real," he "tells it like it is," confronting the daughter with a direct shaming statement,

played for laughs: "What we need you to do is keep your clothes on and go to work everyday." His mock exasperation brings a wave of applause from the audience.

3. On the NBC comedy, *Friends*, one episode features a stripper who comes to a bachelor party for Chandler, sleeps with Joey, and is later accused of stealing the engagement ring from the bedside table. Joey shouts the refrain, "Stripper stole the ring!" In her namelessness, the stripper identity effaces her humanity and covers it up with stereotypes of immorality and misdemeanors. She did not steal the ring after all, they discover, but the focus of the episode remains on the groom and groomsman's anxiety, not on the assumption that the stripper is a thief.

4. In the coverage of a racketeering case against the owner of the Gold Club, a news reporter in Atlanta describes a lawsuit initiated by one exotic dancer for defamation of character, after having been accused of prostitution by the club owner. The reporter ends his segment with a wiseacre aside: "How you can defame a stripper's character—I'll leave you to ponder that." As if the stripper automatically trades her rights to accurate representation by working in this stigmatized profession (and perhaps she does, but she shouldn't have to).

5. Katie Couric interviews Natalie Portman regarding her role as a stripper in the film, *Closer* (2004), and in

> breathy astonishment, Katie exclaims, "Look at you, you're so sweet. Not like a cheesy, sleazy stripper." Natalie explains her research in strip clubs, telling Katie that she discovered a wide variety of women working as strippers, some who feel empowered, others for whom it is a last resort. Despite Natalie's efforts to correct the stereotype, Katie's characterization of the "sleazy stripper" holds its ground as good old mainstream common sense. In this respect, Katie Couric shares something with the worst segment of strip-club customers: a basic belief in the dirtyness and subhumanity of strippers.

It is this belief that shapes the narrative arc of most film and television portrayals of strippers, many of which are punctuated by the stripper's death, a point to which I return in more detail below. In this way, media representations of strippers literalize the metaphor of slut bashing, often subjecting stripper characters to excessively violent ends, the same fate that has awaited all marginalized femininities in media culture, from prostitutes to lesbians to the sexually active teen heroines in horror films ("sluts die first," as poet Daphne Gottlieb reminds us in *Final Girl*).[49]

While I am aware of the complex debates over the causal relationship between images of violence and violence in "real" life, I want to bracket that conversation in order to create a link between violence against sex workers and another form of hate crime, between slut bashing and gay bashing. From this vantage point, films that climax with a stripper death or prostitute rape can be seen as part of a larger framework of violence against and disciplining of sexual minorities. Any time a post-gay rights show thematically addresses gay bashing, from the attacks on Justin and Darren on Showtime's *Queer as Folk* to the award-winning film about Brandon Teena, *Boys Don't Cry,* to the documentary about Mathew Shepard, *The Laramie Project,* it is clear that the intention is to raise consciousness about the problem of gay bashing. This presents a marked difference from representations of violence against sex workers. Whereas the queer community has made bashing a key activist site, there has been far less visible activism within the women's movement against sex-worker bashing, whether it be verbal, ideological, or representational. When a stripper is raped or killed on film or television, it is less clear what the ideological intention of the media text is. The possibility of voyeuristic pleasure, sadistic punishment, or sexist assumptions is a more likely intention and effect than consciousness-raising. My hope here is to make stripper bashing visible in a new way, as analogous to gay bashing, a difficult endeavor since these shows rarely put violence against sex workers in an overtly politicized context in the same way that gay-bashing dramas do. In the same way that murdered or murderous homosexuals have shifted from a common cliché to a site of activist analysis, perhaps the dead sex worker may be harnessed to more progressive media visions of sexuality and presented as a problem rather than an inevitable fate or appropriate punishment. What follows is a first step toward compiling a "necrology" of stripper deaths (with a nod to the necrology section of Vito Russo's *The Celluloid Closet: Homosexuality in the Movies*). These media images are interwoven with scenes from my own life that explore the influences and limitations of this narrative pattern.

RED FEATHER BOA

HBO's original series, *The Sopranos*, features a strip club called the Bada Bing where the gangsters often do business. In most episodes, the club is mere background. Red lights and silicone tits add glitz to the show. But one episode follows the story of an individual dancer named Tracee. She dates Ralphie, a frustrated Soprano crew member, and she entertains delusions of domestic harmony, imagining their lives joining together at the end curve of a New Jersey cul-de-sac. Tracee is offered as pure stereotype: product of a broken home, drug abuser, bad mother. She is infantilized by Silvio, the club manager, who chastises her for fraternizing when she tries to speak with Tony, the mob boss. Later Silvio backhands her after she misses work for several days, slamming her against the car hood with her arm twisted behind her back. Her "shaved twat" belongs to him, he barks, until she pays off her loan for braces. The climactic scene of the episode comes when Tracee calls Ralphie's manhood into question in front of his crew members. She is angry because he has not called in three days, after finding out that she is pregnant with his child. He has no intention of setting up house with her. His official girlfriend is a respectable woman. Tracee is his piece of ass, but she does not recognize her own low status because Ralphie sweet talks her most of the time. As his avoidance of a future with her becomes clear, and Tracee recognizes her position in his life as mere whore, she makes fun of him in self-defense. He follows her outside to the parking lot behind the Bada Bing where they argue. He calls her a cocksucking slob, and she slaps him. Long story short, he retaliates in dramatic excess, punching her in the face, then bashing her head against the guardrail thirteen times. In this gruesome scene, viewers are reminded of what happens to women who venture into strip clubs—that cautionary tale we know so well—how we'll end up in a Dumpster, never to be seen again.

Tracee's death is clearly the intended focal point of the episode, but I want to redirect the audience's eye to a different scene, a less extreme moment in the show, the opening scene of the episode. The camera pans left and down to eye level, resting on an empty wooden stage with a pole at either end. Melancholy guitar sounds drift softly overhead as a waitress brings a tray of drinks out. The first stripper enters, crawling on hands and knees across the raised floor, already topless, wearing a strappy black T-bar. Two more enter: one blonde, then a second brunette. The music laments that it "doesn't seem like it matters very much anymore." The lyrics wind around each body, wrap the moment, cotton-dull and lonely. Three topless girls dance onstage in the most mundane of stripper styles: small footwork, some version of the step-ball-change from childhood tap lessons, long hair swishing left to right across the tops of their buttocks, every now and then an around-the-world sweep or forward lean and backward snap, back arched, hair flying in orchestrated cascades. Just enough motion to remind customers they are in the presence of live women and not flat magazine pages, not enough to disturb the trancelike projections of desire across the blank screen of girl bodies onstage. Three girls, three sets of breasts, three slight variations on the same moves, show ponies tossing their manes and clip-clopping around in platform heels, taking turns at center pole, handing it off like the bar in a relay race. The dancer looks down her own body, directing the customer's gaze away from the eyes, pushing his attention down around the ankles, stepping back out of it. She showcases the flesh, lightly grazing bare abdomen and pelvic cage as if an invisible drink has spilled down the front, checking to see if it will stain, or like freshly done fingernails held carefully away from clothes, layers of loud acrylic still wet. The lurid red light bathes these girl bodies in tones of danger, spotlighting the strip-club stage as a forbidden zone, inviting our eyes to indulge in this stigmatized spectacle.

What I notice, though, is that the third stripper wears a red boa. But her feminine play is obscured by the camera's gaze and the script, both focused elsewhere, on a conversation among men, the principle players. The girls seem almost irrelevant, part of the decor, certainly not the center of attention for the characters or the audience. It would be interesting to reimagine this generic opening scene from the strippers's perspective, using the popular convention in contemporary women's literature of retelling a story from the minor/female character's vantage point. "I've been on that stage," writes Nicole Grasse, "and it's hard for me to watch without imagining her thoughts." In "Tales of a Tokyo Stripper," an ex-dancer named Alison is interviewed about stereotypes of sex workers she'd like to see dispelled, and she responds to the distortions created by the media's pervasive male-centered gaze:

> [W]hen you see strip clubs in movies, the story is always about some guy and strip clubs are just this place that men go to have their fun. Strippers are bimbos. Then the guy leaves and that's the end of that segment. Well, now that I've been a stripper, I identify with the bimbos.

Alison's answer hits the pause button on the VCR, lingers over stripper cameos long enough to consider how much more there might be to the narrative if we followed her offstage, listened to her interact with her co-workers, watched her go home, remove her mascara, watch reruns on TV. How might Tracee or one of the other nameless strippers have narrated this episode of *The Sopranos*? What other scenes might we have seen? I'd like to get *more* of the story of the red boa—when it was bought, what the dancer said or thought as she took it out of her locker and draped it around her shoulders, how it made her feel about herself as she looked in the mirror, so tan and exotic and playful—and *less* of the predictable verbal denigrations, drug-addled stereotypes, and jaw-dropping violence.

When Tony flies into a rage at the sight of Tracee's dead body, Ralphie excuses himself for his bad behavior by shouting that she was a whore. Tracee's status—as stripper, mistress, or prostitute—is low on the gangster scale of valuable womanhood. She moves among categories, blurring the line between girlfriend and sex worker. Earlier in the episode, the camera pans her lovely naked body, with Ralphie penetrating her from behind and a uniformed cop pushing his penis into her mouth. In this scene she could easily be read as a prostitute, and in the Bada Bing the strippers often shift between exotic dancer and prostitute. The bouncer tells a new dancer the drill: fifty dollars to get into the back room where the gangsters party, plus a blow job for him later. It is important to belabor the fact of this slippage between kinds of sex workers on *The Sopranos* for two reasons. First, in my experience as a stripper, the move from one level of sex work to another is rare. Women tend to define themselves by the kind of sex work they would or would not do: bikini bar, topless only, nude but no touching, lap dancing, peep show, call girl, streetwalker. For this reason, I would distinguish the representation of Tracee as stripper/whore from real live strippers I have known or been. Strippers on *The Sopranos* may be whores, but that says more about media mythologies about sex work than it does about the labor conditions of strippers. This is not to deny the possibility of managerial coercion to participate in prostitution, but to create some distance between the identities of stripper and prostitute. Perhaps it's a flimsy distinction since the prostitute is no more appropriate a target for violence than the stripper. The point here is that to say that a stripper is a whore is one way this culture justifies violence against strippers. In almost every case, media representations of strippers show them agreeing to some form of sex for money, tapping into whore hatred as a source and explanation for the violence they endure.

Second, I am unconvinced that Tracee sees herself as a prostitute. In the double penetration scene, she could easily be performing as girlfriend rather than as sex worker, seeking to please the man she hopes to marry, showing off her talent and stamina, lending out her body as material through which Ralphie can claim higher status in his blue-collar masculinity. With these two reservations about casting Tracee as a prostitute in mind, Ralphie's description of her as a whore, echoed relentlessly on *The Sopranos* discussion board, emerges as an important factor in constructing a narrative about Tracee that permits him to kill her. One viewer demands, "Why the uproar over a dead whore?" Hardening against emotional involvement, another viewer points a smug finger at Tracee, writing, "When people work in places like that they deserve whatever they get."[50]

ASKING FOR IT

Picture me, age twenty-two, lying on a couch in the middle of the night, listening to Mazzy Star's *So Tonight That I Might See* on the

CD player's infinite repeat and waiting out a bad acid trip. Upstairs, my stripper friend, Ivy, sleeps next to her stripper boyfriend, Virgo. I guess they were used to bad acid because they turned in early, leaving me to imagine the slow strychnine assault on my organs, rat poison drawing me up in a ball. Everyone knows that problems always seem worse at night, but that's nothing compared to how frightening life looks on cheap acid. Earlier in the evening I'd seen Ivy and Virgo snorting cocaine and selling little packages of it to their stripper friends who dropped by. I had been away at school for a year and my impression on this visit was that they had gotten more deeply involved in drugs during that time. The previous summer we all worked together at a club in Atlanta, and after work we sometimes did drugs recreationally, but it felt like we were dabbling, just being kids. Now they seemed hardcore with skinny bodies and wide pupils. I felt my insides curl up when the two of them dove for the floor after one platinum blonde left with her new purchase.

"Did you see the rock that fell out of her nose?" they gasped in delight.

"No," I said, masking my horror. I'd never seen anyone pick through shag carpet for a rock of cocaine that fell out of another person's nose before. It freaked me out. I wondered if I was staying in a crack house.

After they went to bed, my paranoia threatened to undo me. Ivy had regaled me with what she must have imagined to be an entertaining tale about a night in the recent past when a guy burst into their apartment brandishing a big gun over some drug-related conflict. She told me this laughing, like it was a comedy of errors, like I was supposed to laugh too. But when I pictured the scene, it was all gore and gun triggers and no one to call for help. I tried to distract myself with Hope Sandoval's soothing voice, but I kept imagining these long-haired stripper-gangster-murderers kicking down the door and machine-gunning the living room where I pretended to sleep, and I knew that if died there that night, the world would not care even a little bit. Just another strung-out stripper done in by the lifestyle she chose. Just another dead stripper. What did she expect? My work as a graduate student, my upper-middle-class family of doctors, nurses, pharmacists—none of that would matter. The story of the stripper—sexual woman, dirty drifter, low-class drug user—would march ahead of me, blotting out any complexity, personal history, or Sunday school attendance records I might hold.

Like Nicole Grasse, of *Salon* magazine, I felt the pressure of *the* stripper story bearing down on me:

> I kept half-expecting to end up like some foolish victim in a made-for-TV movie. If I ended up dead or raped somewhere, wouldn't I have been asking for it? I could imagine my life summed up in a few paragraphs in the paper: Stripper disappears, stripper's body found. It was as though by entering that world, I had consented to any abuse I might get. Although I understood intellectually it was wrong, I couldn't shake the sense that somehow, by entering this world, I was asking for it.

Indeed, most people accept violence against strippers as a natural part of the job, to be expected, like being in the military and going to war. The risk is seen as a price one pays willingly, a choice one makes, a danger one knows going in. This society goes further out of our way to protect highway workers than whores, posting signs along the road: "Let them work. Let them live." Sex workers remain outside the boundaries of those who can reasonably expect safe work environments, much less respect or right wages. The persistent link between sex work and danger comes across as natural, but this expectation mystifies the ideological work of the link. It is a load-bearing wall in the social construction of proper femininity. It needs to come down. My night sweats resulted not from the inherent dangers of hanging around strippers, but from the fact that our cultural devaluation of stripper lives left me feeling unprotected by the usual network of social controls.

THE PERFECT STRIPPER

In writing about media images of strippers, I find it difficult to achieve an appropriately complex tone and stance. I don't want to be the humorless feminist, the one who doesn't get the joke. I don't want to be the media police. I would much rather write about what I like in media culture, how much I appreciate *The Sopranos* for the very fact that strip-club culture operates as an everyday backdrop. However, the ubiquitousness and extremity of stripper bashing needs to be cataloged because strippers move through the world with the burden of these images in our minds and the ideas they plant in our customers and family members. On *Six Feet Under*, a prostitute named Melissa comments on the overdetermined dead-whore story. When one of the main characters, Brenda, informs Melissa that she will be writing about her in a thinly veiled novel, Melissa tells her to go ahead as long as she doesn't end up raped or murdered. "I am so sick of that story," she announces. I, too, am sick of that story, and in documenting it, I am aware of the ironic effect of reiterating the very thing I wish to oppose.[51]

Instead of simply saying again that sexual women are often punished in literature and mass media, I want to put pressure on the story, figure out how it functions, what it does for our culture in this particular moment. When a dark comedy like *Very Bad Things* (2002) uses the absurdly exaggerated trope of the stripper death to initiate its plot and support its themes of marriage, loss of control, and betrayal, it is worth considering why the image of a stripper impaled on a bathroom-wall hook functions as the perfect combination of funny and horrific. What does it mean to categorize stripper bashing as a "very bad thing" if you are speaking tongue in cheek? Sharon Willis describes a similar idiom of humor in her analysis of Quentin Tarantino's films:

> To be caught laughing when something horrific happens, gasping at the mismatch between our affective state and the next image, reproduces or recalls the embarassment, or even shame, of being caught in a breach of social discipline. Tweaking our internal social censorship mechanisms through such uncomfortable intersections of the funny and the horrifying, these films leave us to manage that affective excess, which we may do by turning shock into embarrassment, or by taking satisfaction in the alibi they provide for us to get away with laughing when we should not.[52]

By casting the strippers' death as a "very bad thing," the film provides the viewer with an alibi to get away with laughing at the morally corrupt and politically incorrect scene of the stripper's corpse suspended on the wall and the subsequent plot direction of dismembering the body and dumping it in the desert. The director, Peter Berg, pinpoints the original seed for the script in his own observations at a bachelor party:

> I came into this party and these girls were doing a sex show on the floor and the guys were being worked into an absolute frenzy. They all started to move in closer and closer to these two girls and the vibe got really weird. And really intense. I sort of sat back and watched this and I wondered what would happen—it started getting tribal—and I wondered what would happen if these guys just snapped. . . . Seeing these guys at this party, I started wondering, what would happen if they went crazy and just attacked these women? An all-out feeding frenzy and before you know it, you've got two skeletons and these guys are eating the women. (Pride n.p.)

My question for Berg, if I were interviewing him, would be: What turned this intense vibe into the stuff of comedy? What turned this vision of frenzy into farce? Berg's description of the contrast between the characters' background—"Nice-looking normal guys, went to college, love their families, go home for Christmas and Thanksgiving, pay their credit card bills, wear Gap clothes, Dockers, play golf"—and the situation of needing to dispose of a stripper's body does not fully answer the question for me. Berg seems to be laughing at the improbability of such a situation, a sense of "outrageousness" that sounds like class bias on his part, not an accurate understanding of the potential for sex and violence in middle-class men's lives. He indicates the Buddhist tenet, "Life is suffering," as a key theme in this film, but it is worth noting the wide gap between the existential suffering of the male characters and the metal hook in the back of the stripper's head.

I want to stand and gawk at the video box in my hand: "She was the perfect stripper for a bachelor party. There was only one problem. She was dead." The word, "What?!," forms in my mouth, my lips the shape of sharp indignation. I know that the movie is not "about" the stripper's death. It is "about" the dynamics of friendship under pressure. It is "about" a bachelor's wedding-eve anxiety. I know I am supposed to let the reel keep rolling, take the dead stripper in stride, as it is so obviously a moment of cinematic overkill, the movie winking at itself in self-conscious play. But my eye catches on the equation of phrases: "the perfect stripper" and "dead." I could write it all off as familiar literary allusion, a revisitation of Edgar Allan Poe, who believed the best subject of poetry was the death of a beautiful woman, or Alfred Hitchcock's famous instruction for good cinema: "Torture the women!" The misogyny of this box copy is noteworthy, but there is something more specific here, a threat aimed at sex workers. This raven-haired Asian woman, on an out-call for a bachelor party in a hotel room in Vegas, goes into the bathroom to fuck one of the groomsmen and ends up with a tube of metal jammed through her body as he bangs her against the wall. Something is askew with this equation, and I begin to wonder if the syntax is backward. Is it that she is the perfect stripper, except she's dead, or is it that she's dead and therefore the perfect stripper? Non-sex worker women can too easily disengage from this misogynist representation, not seeing it as relating to them at all. The humor works because a large segment of the audience makes a morality distinction (good and bad characters, deserving or not deserving what they get) rather than merely a gender distinction. Stripper sexuality offers a comfortable target for men and women to demonize and castigate together. The comedy of errors sobers me once again.

HOT PINK BIKINI

Gil is driving Nikki and me to a fraternity party near Cornell. I don't know why Nikki invites me to be her partner at these parties. I don't look the part. I am a graduate student at Binghamton, and I make a point during my shifts at the strip club to "trouble" the stripper identity. I have very short hair, no acrylic nails, no boob job. I am not blonde or particularly tan. I rarely wear pink. A friend of mine looked at some nude photographs of me, all artsy in black and white against a background of northern woods in winter, and she determined that I looked like a greyhound. Concave, arched. Nothing voluptuous or bouncy or MTV beach party. But Nikki teamed up with me anyway, and I kept thinking I'd stumble on the right party where I could make the quick thousand strippers are purported to tally in an evening. Nikki moved like honey, and if anyone could get the dollars rolling it was her.

We stay upstairs in a dingy room, drinking Crown Royal and tying on neon bikinis until the pledges have been blindfolded. We are there to tease these young men, to aid in their humiliation in front of their older fraternity brothers. Nikki starts on one end of the circled folding chairs and I start on the other. At the strip club we cannot touch the customers, but here we grind in their laps, first facing them, then facing away. We bend over, push our buttocks against their thin college-boy chests. They are wearing button-down shirts and ties, the aesthetic of aspiring middle management. They are all drunk. After we've made the rounds, the older brothers instruct the pledges to remove their blindfolds. A couple of them howl. Others snicker like little boys. I am never at ease in these scenarios, always wondering what on earth to do next, how to fill the time in the most entertaining way, how to mask my uncertainty. I want them to see me as a stripper tonight, not a smartass grad student who couldn't be bothered to get her nails done. Nikki, on the other hand, has no such concerns. She comes over to me and suggests that we play some games to make more money. The first game requires a volunteer willing to spend a twenty. He must lie in the middle of the floor with the twenty folded lengthwise and placed on his face. I let Nikki go first on this one. She stands over him, lowers herself to his face, grinds his nose in her crotch until I wonder if it hurts him, then picks up the bill by clenching her butt cheeks together. I am a quick study. Soon I have a twenty between my legs as well. We encourage the brothers to cover one of their pledges in five-dollar bills. They unzip his pants and tuck one halfway through the zipper. They open his shirt and put fives on his nipples. In this game the trick is simply to pick up the fives with our mouths, and we linger tantalizingly over the sensitive areas while the crowd hoots and jeers.

Finally, the requisite lesbian scene. Gil, acting as our bouncer, clears the middle of the floor, pushing the guys back to give us a respectable amount of room. We hand him fists of crushed bills for us to divvy up later, and he retreats to the doorway. Nikki lies down, and I crawl toward her. She is sexy, and I don't mind putting my face against her thighs. We simulate all the familiar porn poses: missionary, cunnilingus, sixty-nine. We kiss with our tongues. I put whipped cream on her nipples and lick it off. I feel comfortable with Nikki because we are friends and because we have actually been to bed together a couple of times. I feel comfortable with the frat guys because I am college-educated and I see them as peers. I teach guys like this every day in my classroom, as a graduate instructor. We share a middle-class background and a certain set of mores. What I don't realize until this moment is that they don't know we share these things. I have stepped outside the recognizable role of peer or good woman, and they soon remind me of this rift. The guys get loud, start pushing into the circle where Nikki and I are doing our show. They get too close, too flip. I feel hands, smell sweat, sense danger. They get coarse. "Yeah, fuck her!" "Suck her tits!" "Let *me* fuck her!" I look at Nikki's perfect body lying beneath me and wonder if they might actually try to fuck us. The circle gets smaller and smaller. Soon Gil calls the party to an end. The guys are acting too rough and we want out. We leave shouting back at them, "Fuck you, too." The middle-class boys in fancy ties have revealed themselves as aggressors, a side I had rarely seen of this type. Once I was categorized as stripper or whore, they were no longer the ones who would protect me.

Gil had been drinking cheap wine all through the party. He drove too fast, and he and Nikki got into a fight. He pushed the car up to one hundred miles an hour. I thought for sure this was the night I was going to die. He pulled over once to yank Nikki out of the car and shut her up. She pulled away from him, leaned her face toward my shoulder and said, "Don't let him get me out of the car." My body jarred through hers by his punches, I thought of getting out of the car, flagging down a ride, calling someone from a convenience store, but we were forty-five miles from home. I was wearing a hot pink bikini under my leather jacket. I did not feel free to roam around looking for a pay phone. Nikki alternately placated and infuriated Gil until he gave her a black eye, which seemed to calm them both down. She whimpered next to me in the backseat, and Gil sped east on

Highway 79. Red and blue lights went off in our back window, and I was relieved that a cop was pulling us over. When he asked Nikki if she was alright, she said she was fine. Worse, I confirmed her story. Between the options of Gil and some anonymous cop in Ithaca, I could not tell which would get me home sooner and safer. I felt something my middle-class background had not prepared me for. I was afraid of the cop. When we got to my apartment building, Nikki jumped out of the car with me, and Gil menaced us on the porch. My landlord came out and threatened to call the police. I blushed when he told me this better not happen again. He's got family to think of. Nikki and I stayed awake all night, listening for the gunning sounds of Gil's car. I felt frightened but righteous, like I was rescuing her, like all the other nights she called me in the next few months, running on the side of the road, bruised and needing a ride. The day after our trip to Ithaca, Nikki went home and Gil gave her a diamond ring. They were engaged.

Is this story about violence against sex workers?

Or is it about violence and heterosexuality?

Cops, frat guys, boyfriends, bouncers—the line between valid fear and paranoia blurs. I can't tell quite where the danger is coming from.

THE FEMINIST REGULAR

Last year I had just started a new job, a real job as a tenure-track professor of English, and two other new hires and I went out for drinks. We were giddy with the new employment. We did shots. It felt good and free and playful, and I suggested, as any sensible person might do in such a moment, that we go to a strip club. Then I burst out laughing, a mix of hilarity and self-loathing, and explained, "Okay, here's what you need to know. Whenever we go out drinking, I will probably at some point suggest that we go to a strip club. But we don't ever really have to go. Just take it as code for 'I'm having fun.' " They agreed to read it as such.

I do this half-in half-out dance as a scholar-stripper. I don't hide the fact that I used to work as a stripper, but I don't introduce myself as Lisa-Johnson-who-used-to-be-a-stripper. I know that the world I live in, the intellectual circles I travel in, will permit some eccentricity, and that few colleagues would respond with audible shock. However, the twin reactions of muted horror and exuberant sensationalization give me little incentive to share. The surprise that students and co-workers have expressed, even when it is mild or delighted surprise, still evinces the remaining stereotypes of women: that we can be the studious bookworm in horn-rimmed glasses or we can be the airheaded sex kitten, all boobs, blonde highlights, and blow jobs. Mind or body. I worked at a strip club during graduate school in part to reconnect these parts of myself, the smart part and the sexy part, the overachiever and the underworld slummer, honor roll and body roll. I have experienced my career as student and professor both as a liberation from the constricting frames of reference provided to me by church and family, and as the ideological state apparatus described by Marxist theorist, Louis Althusser, in which school is one among a number of sites through which individuals are "cramm[ed] . . . with daily doses of nationalism, chauvinism, liberalism, moralism."[53] When the university campus begins to feel like another space where you have to perform a gender- and class-appropriate identity, embodying the ideologically conservative discourses of respectability, it is no wonder that a woman with feminist inclinations might need an infusion of carnivalesque nonrespectability.

The exhortation to "respect yourself" is used throughout women's lives to discipline their sexual behaviors (don't have sex out of marriage, don't sleep with too many partners, don't sleep with more than one partner at a time, don't wear your lipstick so red, don't show so much cleavage, don't, don't, don't, don't, don't). It's enough to make a girl want to climb on a stage and take off her clothes. Or, after a certain age, go watch other women do just that.[54]

Now that I don't strip anymore, I enjoy an occasional night out at a gentleman's club. I am glad there are public spaces devoted to eroticism, nudity, titillation, and loud bass. I love to pick out a sexy lady and pay her to dance topless between my open legs—to sit at a table near the stage, sip whiskey, and indulge in brief crushes on selected house girls. I fall fast for "Ireland," with her short, blonde, spikey hair and black fishnet bikini, or "Jennifer," with a chestnut bob and teal spandex, circling their hips and running fingertips along the edge of each curve and dip.

I feel no qualms about patronizing these businesses, even though my experience as a stripper is marked in my memory by mixed feelings. I watch the women dance and wonder how their evenings are going, whether they've made tip-out yet, how hard they've had to hustle for it, and then I invite them over to my table. I remember my frustration as a dancer when young men in baseball caps held out a dollar and instructed me to turn around for them, to "work for it," and I am glad to offer a break from disrespectful customers. I had to train myself to be comfortable opening my legs so the dancer could perform between my knees, the socialization of femininity embedded in my automatic gesture of crossed legs, one knee hooked tightly over the other.

I know that some of my revelations in this essay may seem shocking to colleagues and family members. It is unusual for a college professor to narrate her own "limit experiences," to borrow a term from Foucault. Bare nipples and bald confessions still jar the academic world. In a recent visit back home, my grandma and I were looking at pictures of me in high school: red hair one year, blonde the next, then black. She said, "I think you liked to shock people." My first response, flustered and defensive, was, "Some people need shocking." Several hours later I figured out what I really meant. I never made decisions about my appearance—or my sexuality, or my sex work, or my sex writing—based on a desire to shock people. I just wanted to live in a world where people were less easily shocked. Writing about the thrill and terror of my experiences as a stripper is part of this effort to imagine a world less easily shocked. Drawing together my feminist identity and my practices as a regular is another part of the same effort, an insistent reconciliation of seemingly opposed desires.

A decade has passed since I first ventured into a strip club and asked for a job, but I am still rereading my body against the texts of this space.[55]

12

Stripper Chic: A Review Essay

Allison Fensterstock

On a fine spring day when I should be outdoors enjoying what passes for fresh air in New Orleans, I'm kicking back on a friend's couch enjoying the luxury of cable television. What's on is a BET "best of" comedy special where, at the moment, a fat white guy is doing a hilarious-ish comparison between the moves and attitudes of white and black strippers respectively. The consensus is that black strippers are better. That's a matter of opinion, but the interesting thing here is the fact that the racially mixed studio audience of urban twenty-and-thirty something folks with all the visual trappings of the professional class are cracking up and nodding knowingly (*It's funny, 'cause it's true!*) in the way that stand-up comedy audiences are wont to do. Strippers and strip clubs have become so normalized in mainstream American culture—at least that which is represented by the programming on basic cable—that the audience gets the joke. This isn't HBO *Real Sex* at midnight. It's a general-interest basic subscriber package cable channel, and it's four o'clock in the afternoon.

Signs of stripper chic have been cropping up since Motley Crue's seminal *Girls, Girls, Girls* video more than ten years ago, but lately they've been increasing almost exponentially. From the mass audience films *Striptease* and *Showgirls* to HBO's *G-String Divas* (a stripper reality show) to the inexplicable popularity of the thong as everyday undies (with its own panty liner!) to the ubiquitous in-house pole on MTV's *Cribs*, the signifiers of the professional naked lady are everywhere. Beyonce Knowles's performance during the TV broadcast of the Essence Awards included a demonstration of what can only be characterized as stripper floor work; she even did that move where you sit on the floor, kick your legs straight up together and swing them individually in circles from the knee to offer tantalizing glimpses of booty. Nelly's bounce anthem "Hot in Herre" includes the line "I got a friend with a pole in the basement." Chandler's routine postbreakup strip club visits were a recurring joke on *Friends*. Pamela Anderson's animated show *Stripperella* (in which a cartoon Pam as stripper/superhero "dances at night, and fights crime later at night" will be one of the first new offerings from the revamped lad-network Spike TV (neè TNN). And, of course, there's Britney's notorious MTV Video Music Awards striptease, and the entire oeuvre of Christina Aguilera. This is way more than stripper chic. It's stripper saturation.

But the most interesting aspect of the entire phenomenon—without which, I think, you could make a case for writing off the whole trend as just another gloriously vulgar expression of America's lust affair with the glamour of trashiness—is the spate of books on the industry by sex workers, academics, and former-sex-worker academics that have popped up over the past few years.

New York Times writer Alex Kucynski writes it off as "what cocaine and models were to fiction in the 1980s and Prozac . . . to the 1990s—obligatory references in works aspiring to urban realism," in a November 2001 piece entitled "The Sex Worker Literati." What Kuczynski and other critics noting the trend, however, fail to notice is the thread of self-examination and feminist awareness running through the work. It's not tit-lit, the kind of tawdry *True Confessions* stuff published to evoke a naughty thrill in the guise of a moral lesson. These books—ranging from the overtly political works that started appearing in the late 1980s to the memoirs (Lily Burana's *Strip City,* Elisabeth Eaves' *Bare*), cultural studies (Katherine Liepe-Levinson's *Strip Show,* Brian McNair's *Striptease Culture*), and anthropological works (Katherine Frank's *G-Strings and Sympathy,* a study of club customers) coming out of the past three years—assume (as opposed to argue for) stripping and other sex work as legitimate labor, however marginalized. The authors also all self-identify as feminist and refrain from passing moral judgment on the industry while still giving a realistic—that is, including the crappy nights—view of their own experiences as sex workers. It's extreme work, but it's not "extreme" literature, and it's being marketed toward—and selling to—the same kind of audience that was knowingly chuckling at the BET comic and his stripper jokes. Mr. and Ms. Average Urban Sophisticate.

The initial round of sex-industry discussion, probably starting with the essay collection *Sex Work* (Delacoste & Alexander, ed., 1987) tended to stay in the reasonably outside-the-mainstream circles of feminist academia and politicized sex workers. At that time, activist organizations like PONY (Prostitutes of New

York), BAYSWAN (Bay Area Sex Workers Advocacy Network), the Exotic Dancers Alliance and the mama of them all, COYOTE (Call Off Your Old Tired Ethics, founded in 1973) had been working steadily to create a support and advocacy network for sex workers *by* sex workers, not well-meaning helpers of the unfortunate. Then, of course, came the feminist for-or-against porn debate polarized by the extreme stances of prominent theorists like Andrea Dworkin (against) and Camille Paglia (very much for), the in-your-face radicalized sexuality of Riot Grrl and the rise of the term "sex-positive feminism."

Sex Work utilizes the form of a loose collection of voices. The text is a compilation of short pieces of fiction, essays, interviews, and poetry on varying sex work-related topics: the actual logistics of the work, activism, political organization, documentation of work-related discrimination and so on. This mirrors the popular third wave feminist text style à la Seal Press: the anthology of personal essays that serves to show the emerging new face of the movement as not a homogenized bloc of sisterhood but a multiplicity of unique voices. In the sex-worker books, this technique presents the reality of the industry much the same way. 1997's *Whores and Other Feminists* is a similar type of collection, as is 2002's *Jane Sexes It Up,* an anthology of writing on feminist sexuality and desire that includes several musings on sex work. Wendy Chapkis's *Live Sex Acts* (1997) uses a variation on the form (mostly interviews) to argue in favor of social acceptance, and across-the-board legalization and regulation of sex work to improve the quality of life for the workers.

The new breed of sex-worker writing is pretty much best exemplified by work that came out in the past year or so: Burana and Eaves's memoirs, dancer Katherine Frank's *G-Strings and Sympathy* based on her doctoral dissertation in cultural anthropology,

McNair's *Striptease Culture* (an examination of the porno-fication of contemporary culture) and Katherine Liepe-Levinson's *Strip Show,* a look at, well, the strip show in terms of its cultural place and meaning. And to my count (source: Amazon.com), ten other nonfiction books relating to some branch of the sex industry.

One notable thing is that in the new books, the world of sex work is no longer such a dark, exotic otherland. Rather, they present the sex industry and sex-worker-chic as a mainstreamed, normal (if somewhat interesting, otherwise they wouldn't write a book about it) aspect of contemporary Western culture. They're not studying it by itself, but how it fits (with the presumption that it *does* fit) into our popular-cultural frame of reference. The other interesting thing is that the fabulous writin' strippers (Burana, Eaves, Frank again, and many of the women who contributed to the earlier sex-work anthologies) are, in shorthand, *nice girls*. Mostly nice middle-class white girls with a college or graduate education (and Burana was immersed in the politically charged community of 1990s punk) and a family they portray as perfectly pleasant. They were members of a certain class—through birth or education—for whom sex work was not an immediately present job option, at least not as is commonly thought. The question isn't necessarily why they chose sex work. That's an easy one to get out of the way, at least on the surface. Q: What's a nice girl like you doing in a place like this? A: Making bank. I think the question is why choose to *write* about it—as in, go public. And, of course, why, since these books aren't one-handed reads, why are they selling, and to serious critical acclaim?

Well, as we've seen, sex work—partly through being made visible by the books that laid the groundwork for the acceptance of these recent ones—is no longer viewed as quite *so* marginal and transgressive in our culture. Since Courtney Love admitted to shaking her moneymaker, it's downright hip in some circles, although whether this new popularity is a backlash against the stereotype of second wave feminism as antisex(iness) or a step forward into a more varied and open feminist movement probably remains to be seen. Also, stripping is a young girl's game and leads to a premature taking-stock. Eaves and Burana's books were both precipitated by a return to stripping after moving on to journalism careers with the express purpose of figuring out what is was all about, what made them do it in the first place, how having done it had made them who they were, and how, which points to the idea that there *is* a little more to it than the Benjamins after all.

The tail end of the 1980s and early to mid-1990s saw a radical shift in the personality of the strip club. This was the dawn of the "gentleman's club" era—clubs like the Scores, Scarlett's, and Rick's Cabaret (publicly traded on NYSE) chains, redesigned with the intent of attracting the wealthy, middle- to upper-class customer in the persona of an upscale social environment with cigars, extensive wine lists and superpremium liquor, fine dining, access to sports scores and stock-market reports, a total guise of respectability—oh, and naked ladies. Lovely, refined naked ladies you could hang out with, drink expensive wine, even "go out to dinner" with in the club, and who might then be asked to show you their boobies. Weirdly enough, the rise of such clubs mirrored the boom in the "lad mags" (*Maxim* et al) who were basically cheeky little brothers to *Playboy* in every aspect but the showing of bare nipple and pubic hair, and so could pose as "respectable" magazines. In essence, the new gentleman's club was a fantasy dating zone with none of the perils of genuine attempts at connection with women in the "real world," where women far out of your league would approach you, reaffirm your heterosexuality, let you relax outside the confusing and changing world of gender relations, and then basically disappear from your life until you choose to return. A "gendered combination of service, leisure, and entertainment" (Frank).

The new, mainstreamed strip club (which often, according to Frank and Liepe-Levinson, is situated in perfectly decent neighborhoods well outside a red-light district sort of area) presented a less transgressive *space* for women to do this in, where they might not have made the leap to dance somewhere overtly "sleazy." (Burana began her naked career in the dearly departed heart of sleaze, Times Square; however, she notes the change in the clubs' personalities in her text and professes shock and joy at trappings like the hair and makeup ladies provided at one of the new breed of clubs, as well as the utter oddness of the "upscale" guyland paradise atmosphere). Eaves comments on the rising trendiness of strip clubs, which is also a central subject in McNair's study of a pornofied mass culture. Nice, normal men patronize strip clubs where nice, normal girls dance. Frank mentions being introduced onstage as a graduate student as matter-of-factly as the DJ might note another dancer's *Playboy* pictorial.

Obviously, the redecoration of the stripper industry was a marketing technique and not intended to create a more pleasant workplace for strippers, but it may have indirectly affected the palatability of the industry for the sort of woman who might be in the position to write a book about it. The brand characteristics of the "new" gentlemen's club also demanded the type of dancer who could believably perform the kind of upper-class personality that would fit in such an environment, which actually ruled out the possibility of employment there for many women from disadvantaged backgrounds and created a job niche for more educated or otherwise privileged potential strippers.

Plus, the rise of sex-positive feminism à la Susie Bright combined with the vicious punk girliness of Riot Grrl had carved out a space, however contested or tenuous, in the breadth of the movement for the concept of the feminist sex worker. Sex workers were becoming the issue of the moment in some feminist circles. However, what Burana calls the "Paglian caricature" of the always-triumphant stripper-goddess rejoicing on her pedestal is somewhat extreme. Making money off of your own naked prettiness (and sticking it to the patriarchy via their wallets) as empowering is arguable but slightly twisted. Rather, I think the ever-emerging cultural presence of the feminist stripper is a manifestation of the ongoing third-wave struggle to banish the demons of forced feminine looks and behaviors as well as the (necessary) rejection of all of those signifiers of femaleness by the second wave. A major project in third wave feminism seems to be the reclaiming of *girliness*—trappings of femininity that are all the more fascinating because they are no longer so required—which include the presentation of the girlie self as an erotic creature with all the struggle implied in this project when you're also trying to retain/find sexual agency and your own preferred mode of sexual expression and self-presentation in a world fraught with peril for ladies in fuck-me shoes and red lipstick.

Making your money off of your feminine charms (including looks *and* wiles) puts what it really means to be female, culturally, in stark relief. And sometimes this no-nonsense look at gender roles and social value is a help, in a world full of confusing messages. The blurb excerpted for the back cover of *Bare* reads in part: "Everyone has an opinion on what to do with female bodies, and sometimes it feels as if the only people who get in trouble for holding such opinions are young women themselves. Some of us, though, have to live in them, and we each get by in our own way." She comments in an early chapter that being looked at sexually in everyday life was something she had come to live with, though not particularly understand. Frank takes it a step further by stating that "through dancing, [she] developed a *feminist ethos of femininity*" that gave her a certain power and understanding of the "idea of performing gender," which in turn imparted a certain freedom. Stripping is a part of the sex industry that is infrequently directly about the sex act (Frank, McNair), and as mentioned above, is often a space for pleasurable, even therapeutic playacting of simplified gender roles—what Stacy Reed (*Whores and Other Feminists*) calls a "clearly defined, consensual area for this behavior"—for the customers. Even Roland Barthes, in his short essay "striptease," considers the strip show to be a necessary "vaccine" of eroticism in a prescribed space, the better to preserve the status quo and inoculate a culture against the unchecked spread of forbidden behaviors into inappropriate contexts. The constant validation of your value through cash is also encouraging in such a space where it would be disturbing in "the real world." What two things are more valued in America, after all, than physical attractiveness and financial success? This kind of "empowerment"—what Funari refers to as the "E" word for its overuse in feminist discourse on sex work—is overly simple as an end in itself, but it definitely serves as a jumping-off point in understanding the popularity of stripper lit. It's not too crazy to suggest that this freedom to act out might be beneficial for the dancers as well, if more obliquely.

Sex work historically has not been just a job; it's a whole experience in the system of class in America. Nina Hartley, in fact, notes that her entry into the porn world was beneficial for her as a feminist because of the exposure to women of varied social classes. In fact, few other fields probably offer the opportunity to gain common experience with such a diverse community of women. Choosing to earn money off of your body (or the idea of your body, as with stripping) also automatically places you in a "lower-class" context, which makes the middle-class girl's choice to dance and go public about it quite interesting. Is this class slipping a matter of slumming? Solidarity? Exposure to class hierarchies? Wendy Chapkis quotes a dancer at San Francisco's Lusty Lady peep show on this class drop as imparting "the freedom of being a leper," with the idea that being outside of respectable society allows a certain latitude in terms of acceptable behavior. Eaves comments, "When I entered the pink-and-red stripperland, my departure [from the moral norm] became official. Having given up the old norms I needed new ones, and where none were provided, I had to make up my own." Frank points out that the performance of bad-girl sexuality inside the club actually doesn't come of as particularly transgressive to the customers; of course you're naughty. You're a stripper. So you have the attendant privilege (requirement, if you want to make any money) of knowingly performing sluttiness and hyperfemininity and actually being rewarded, not punished for it.

If it was *only* about the money, I don't think that experiences of sex work would beg so much self-reflective examination. Why would Burana and Eaves need to return to the business to seek resolution after moving on to other careers otherwise? Why would Erika Langley, whose memoir and photo collection *The*

Lusty Lady came out in 1997, ultimately choose to continue dancing in a peep show after completing the book project that was the impetus for the job in the first place? Why does she refer to a place where come is routinely mopped off the floor as a place that "changed my life . . . and taught me about my own erotic power?"

Several of the recent stripper-lit books (Burana, Frank, and Eaves) include a humorous rundown of popular stripper names and their categories (girl-next-door, animals, gems, food). The names are a campy aspect of stripping that's fun to read about, but the fact that strippers almost always choose a one-word alias designed to attract men, or a certain kind of spendy man, is worth examining. Stripper names serve as shields that illustrate the relief of reducing your work persona to a single, simple thing distant from your genuine self, a self whose real-life gendered sexual behavior is riddled with complications and possible consequences. Eaves writes (referring to living female in "the real world"): "I thought I had a uniquely female fear, this ever-present sense that my sexuality could be used against me." But in stripperland, your performer-self is protected by context. It's performance; you're not *you*. Your stripper self, by virtue of existing solely in an arena where her behavior is condoned and safe, has a certain measure of extra latitude you don't have in the outside world. Behavior that would be punished *out there* is allowed, even rewarded, *in here*. Frank, in her essay, "Working the Pool," muses on the enjoyable dissonance of being nude in public. "Only I am allowed to take my clothes off [referring to customers and other club staff] in public, and only here," she writes.

Eaves and Frank both mention a sensation of freedom that comes, paradoxically, with the job requirement to play girl.

Eaves recalls being spellbound upon her first civilian visit to a strip club; the girls were "free of the straightjacket. They were not only permitted to be ostentatiously sexual, they were celebrated for it . . . they were applauded, glorified, even paid." To accept and own the idea of your own female body as an overt commodity in a safe zone (where the behavior is acceptable and protected by a system of rules, laws, internalized cultural ideas, and big old bouncers) is an act of facing down a taboo that can certainly be "the E-word" in a self-discovery sort of way. It simplifies and strips the fear off of the confusing concept of your body existing in an intricate system of value you did not design, a system full of complicated rules based on how you present yourself intentionally or not as a sexual creature, to just say: "Okay. I'm shaved and painted and nekkid and wriggling around. I'm the ultimate mainstream hetero fantasy girl. This is what you encourage me to be and what you punish me for being, I think. Now pay me." You push the boundaries of girlie sexiness so far you're practically a drag queen. And nothing especially horrible happens to you. Liepe-Levinson quotes feminist writer and stripper Seph Weene on this subject: Weene felt she was "being sexy on purpose, the initiator, not the victim" of her own sexuality. And though your performance persona is separate from "you" in terms of immediate culpability, she shares your body. Her triumphs and knowledge are your own.

The self-awareness necessitated by an act of performance is also important. Luce Irigaray, in the feminist semiological work *This Sex Which Is Not One,* writes that the performance of hyperfemininity, or what Frank calls "doing girl,"—the act of knowingly adopting the behaviors and various accessories of standard hetero fantasy-femininity—turns "a form of subordination into an affirmation." Barthes theorizes that it is the act and accessories of the striptease, not the final product of naked lady that is erotic. He writes, "Woman is desexualized at the very moment when she is stripped naked." It is the signifiers of erotic femininity—the "feathers, furs, and gloves"—that contain the mystery of the sexual female: "It is self-evident law that the whole of striptease is given in the very nature of the initial garment." After dancing, one gains an understanding and power over the cultural performances of femininity. As Frank writes, "Perhaps it is the ability to move among these and other options for womanhood that measure contemporary Western women's feelings of freedom (or lack thereof)." Stripping teaches you not just to "do girl" but to *own* girl.

So, possibly, it's the value of these sneaky lessons absorbed through the business of professional-naked-lady-ness that might be what drives the new stripper literati to reexamine their experiences in the public form of mass-market trade books. I think the way these books treat the experience of sex work certainly points to a new stage in the position of the sex worker within a feminist context. Having a literary canon—a louder and more diverse voice—can only aid a group that has been historically silenced or at least marginalized. The way the books demystify the industry is likely to bring more mainstream attention to it from a sympathetic standpoint, making it more visible and probably aiding the efforts of activist groups who work to improve working conditions and increase social awareness and acceptance of sex work as real pink-collar labor. Already more hip-stripper resources are popping out like the excellent Seattle-based *Danzine* and the online community Stripperweb.com.

The trend can definitely be seen as an expression of the third wave aim to comprise a movement of multiple voices. Because it's so damn marketable, though, (and it might be too late) you have to watch out for what I would call the Spice Girl effect, i.e., the boom in mass-market "girl culture" in the late 1990s that bastardized the complex radical feminism of Riot Grrl into a shorthand of baby barrettes and "Girl Power." Or the overly simplified "Paglian caricature" of the empowered, triumphant sex-bomb-bitch, because all the texts above well demonstrate the potential suckiness of sex work (in no small part because the work requires constantly being pleasant to rude jerks, and because you don't always make nine hundred dollars a night, no matter how hot you are). The phenomenon is definitely ripe for the pitfall of turning into the selling of the baby tee of radical self-realization to the strippified masses without the grounding in the politics, history, and feminist theory that would make it valuable. But the linking of intelligent mainstream-ish voices with the sex industry is likely to ultimately serve to help break down the old cultural Madonna-whore (or professor-whore) dichotomy within feminism and work toward the normalization of an integrated, hot, sexy, self-aware feminist intellect for those who want it.

13

Keeping Her Off the Pole? Creating Sexual Value in a Capitalist Society

Katherine Frank

Comedian Chris Rock has become the father of a baby girl named Lola, and in addition to his jokes about racism, politics, and relationships, he has now added material on fathering. One of his main tasks as a father, he claims in one of his monologues, is to "keep her off the pole." And just to be safe, "My daughter is staying away from all poles, that includes monkey bars," he says. Rock believes that having a daughter who is a stripper is the ultimate failure for a father.[56]

As the mother of a baby girl, and as a former stripper, I found that Rock's comments gave me reason to pause. Certainly, the news headlines and television stories often make me stop to think about how one should go about *educating* kids about sexuality. After all, despite all of the hype about abstinence, kids are experimenting sexually at young ages. Oprah interviews young teens about "salad tossing" (oral-anal sex) and "rainbow parties" (oral sex fests where the girls wear different colors of lipstick). A network news story breaks about a ring of middle-school group sex parties outside a Southern metropolis. A wide range of near-erotica can be viewed on late-night television, and kids are definitely tuning in. Even parents are becoming familiar with the popular terms "fuck buddies" and "friends with benefits," used by youth to denote casual sexual encounters. *Girls Gone Wild* has become a profitable series of videos (*Girls Gone Wild on Campus, Girls Gone Wild Doggy Style, Girls Gone Wild America Uncovered,* etc.) in addition to being used as a description of a regular Saturday night and young girls flash their breasts or butts in exchange for baseball hats, T-shirts, cheap glass beads, or simply a few whistles. NBC conducts a poll on teen sexual attitudes and behaviors and finds that twenty-seven percent had "been with somebody in an intimate or sexual way" (despite the certain denials of their parents), twelve percent had engaged in oral sex, thirteen percent had had sexual intercourse, and that half of those who had engaged in oral sex or intercourse had done so by age fourteen. Religion seems to quell early sexual behavior a bit, but not completely: teens from Protestant and Catholic families were equally likely to be sexually active (twenty-six percent) while teens from nonreligious families were slightly more active (thirty-nine percent).[57] In many of the news stories, unfortunately, it seems that girls are striking unequal bargains: they tend to claim that their exploits are primarily about pleasing the boys and they still tell stories about being judged negatively by those very young men that they are so interested in serving. (*Do you think any of these boys will ask you to the prom? Oprah asks some party girls. The answer: It doesn't bode well for a corsage and dinner*).

My primary concern is actually not about *preventing* my

daughter (or anyone else's) from becoming sexually active early. Such prevention efforts may not be effective or worthwhile. Some kids do begin these explorations at young ages, no matter how their parents try to prevent them, and for many of us who blossomed relatively early, such experience is not necessarily negative. I was personally quite interested in sexual things at an early age and believe that my experimentations during my teen years were important in determining the woman that I would become. On the other hand, I know that I did sometimes engage in sexual activity of different kinds for reasons other than for desire or self-exploration. Sometimes I ended up in a situation because I wanted to be popular, or wanted a particular guy to like me, or didn't want to seem too uptight since my friends were all "hooking up" at the same time. Sometimes I thought, *why not?* and couldn't come up with a good answer. Sometimes I drank too much and made decisions that I later regretted. A lot of us did. And, it seems, a lot of young girls (and boys) still do. Luckily, I had been provided with enough information about sexuality that my regrets were primarily emotional—I did not end up with sexually transmitted diseases, unwanted pregnancies, or with bodily scars from physical violence. These risks are real and youth should be educated about them at multiple forums. Recitations of the "horrors" of sexual activity are not, however, very effective as preventive measures, for some of us.

Clearly, Rock believes that when young girls turn to stripping, or some other form of sex work, it is an example of the widespread tendency to devalue their sexuality, to see themselves simply as objects for men, and to engage in sexual activity and exhibitionism for no good reason. Yet I'm not sure I'd necessarily agree. When I began stripping in my late twenties and met women working in all different areas of the sex industry, I learned things about my sexuality that I believe would have helped me in my earlier years to avoid negative sexual situations. First of all, through stripping I actually learned how incredibly valuable my sexuality was. Not just valuable in terms of female virtue ("be careful not to lose your reputation"), an idea I found fairly nebulous and unconvincing all along (perhaps because I had already lost mine). Instead, I found that my sexuality was tangibly valuable. *Economically* valuable. What I had once given away for free, I learned, men were willing to pay for, and quite highly. This simple realization changed the way I thought about a lot of things, including my decisions to engage in sexual activity or to show off my body for others *outside* of the club. I see cheerleaders now and wonder if they realize how much money they could be making for those peeps up their skirts. I view young girls dressed like Paris Hilton with an almost conservative eye: Why are they going out dressed like that? Why show all that skin for nothing more than a bit of attention? Can't they see that they could be paying off their school loans with such attire and behavior?

In this capitalist context, where sexuality is sold and used to sell in multifarious ways, I don't think a father's greatest failure would be for his daughter to become a stripper. In fact, her choice of jobs could be seen as an intelligent entrepreneurial decision. At least she's not shrugging her shoulders when asked later why she was disrobing onstage in front of men (the way so many spring breakers and Mardi Gras enthusiasts tend to sheepishly do). In his comedy routine, Rock also disputes the idea that girls are stripping to pay for their education: "I haven't heard of a college that takes dollar bills. I haven't seen any clear heels in biology. I haven't ever gotten a smart lap dance." Sure, the comment is meant to be funny, as if strippers would always look like strippers in their five-inch heels and glitter, or show up to pay their tuition with folded money pulled straight from their garters. Yet, what Rock is really saying is that the woman who profits from selling sexual entertainment is not going to be able to accomplish anything else. Fortunately, he is wrong.

Many of my stereotypes were also overturned when I became a stripper and recognized how hypocritical people's judgments of sex workers tended to be. At one time, for example, I believed that prostitutes must be miserable women, that strippers were most certainly exploited, and that porn stars probably had experienced all sorts of psychological trauma. My experiences and friendships in the sex industry made me rethink a lot of these assumptions. I came to understand the sex industry not as a panacea for sexual ills or a capitalist utopia, but as an industry with many of the same benefits and drawbacks as other industries. I began to question why it was that women who sold sex or sexual fantasies were criminalized and stigmatized, while women who gave it away for free were either accepted and valorized (as long as they didn't give away too much, to too many people) or pathologized (if they did give away too much, to too many people or the *wrong* people, or enjoyed it too greatly). Perhaps, I came to believe, we are barking up the wrong tree when we assume that sex or sexual expression has some predetermined meaning or that it necessarily has to be coupled with romantic love (something the college students who are embarking on their one night stands and friends-with-benefits relationships already know). Perhaps, I also came to believe, the distaste that people express when confronted with explicit sex-for-money (or sexuality-for-money) exchanges was also hypocritical, rooted more in ideology and fear than in any truth about sexuality.

One night after a few margaritas and a lot of discussion about raising a beloved daughter in a sexist and sexual world, I wondered aloud to my friends about whether I might suggest that my own daughter sell her virginity on the Internet as some enterprising youngsters have already begun doing. It would give her a reason to save it, I surmised, and perhaps it will be legal to do so in the future. After all, why lose your virginity to some high-school guy in the backseat of a car (or wherever it happens nowadays), while you are drunk or stoned (or whatever kids do to lose their inhibitions nowadays), when you could get paid good money for it? She might earn enough from that one encounter for a down payment on a house, or to buy a new car, or to put away for college tuition. She might like the guy or she might not. Who cares? It would be quick and painless, because she would have the knowledge to make it so. And liking someone can be a transient state anyway—who ends up with the first guy they sleep with in the long term, or even the short term? Probably fewer people than one would expect (or than the abstinence folks are hoping).

After their initial horrified reactions, my friends began to see my point, even dressed as it was in hypothetical attire. One woman remembered feeling as if her virginity was a kind of blight to be gotten rid of as quickly as possible. She had made a bet with her friends to see who could lose it first, and though all of them successfully accomplished their missions right around the same time (not exactly Mission Impossible, after all), the experiences had been uniformly unimpressive. Several women told of wanting their first time "to be perfect," but "settling" for far less. One woman couldn't remember the first time she had sex, as she had downed a pint of whiskey to avoid worrying about the supposedly imminent (but never actually forthcoming) "pain."

Some first-time stories are romantic and some are upsetting and abusive, but most are unexpectedly banal. Certainly, if a young girl was *planning* on socking away some cash for the "gift" of her virginity, she might at least use that sense of value if she decides to be generous and bestow such a gift on a boyfriend. She might negotiate. She might *insist* that he take her on dates, or buy her Valentine's Day presents, talk to her in the halls the next day instead of whispering behind her back with his buddies, or even use a condom—tall orders for some young men nowadays. And, it seems, high expectations for some young women. Perhaps she might even insist on having an orgasm, or at least require him to make some attempt at providing her with sexual pleasure as well. Perhaps she would decide that it was a gift of love, and would request that he accept it in those terms (rather than simply hoping that he might feel the same way someday).

And what about all of those other experiences short of losing one's virginity? How might she feel about those? The quick gropes that were allowed to appease a drunk fraternity boy, the backseat blow jobs (with no reciprocation of any kind), the frantic dry-humping (which does, in fact, often resemble an unpracticed lap dance)? What are those moments worth?

These comments are not offered to feed or stir up any kind of crazy passion for virgins or to suggest that anyone engage in illegal activity. Nor are they meant to suggest that all young women would be served by working in the sex industry. *This is a thought experiment*: the issue at hand is really not whether or not you actually sell your sexuality in some form or another, or give it away for free. The issue is whether or not young girls feel like they *own* their own sexualities. How does one maintain one's own understanding of sexual value in a world where sex is both incessantly commodified, on the one hand, and invested with multiple layers of often contradictory meaning on the other (love, fear, pleasure, sin, freedom, commitment, adventure)? Unfortunately, laws against prostitution mean that, legally, women do not "own" their sexualities outright. We cannot do with our bodies as we see fit in the sexual realm (although we are certainly allowed—even coerced—to sell our bodies for other forms of demeaning labor). Not yet, anyway. However, we can own our sexuality in the sense that we can consciously decide what counts as a good reason for having sex (love, money, pleasure, fame, popularity) or expressing ourselves sexually in other ways and we can still demand respect and care for our bodies from those people we interact with sexually. We might not always get that respect, but we should at least be confident enough in our own sexual value to ask for it. This is something that feminists have fought for over the years, a reward that we hope our children will also be able to reap.

So how will I respond if my daughter becomes a stripper someday? Probably with the same ambivalence that I'd respond to any job choice—they all require some amount of compromise (and as of yet, I can't even imagine her leaving the house on her own so this is *really* becoming a thought experiment). Certainly, I could imagine that stripping would teach her the value of her body, as it did for me; that it is acceptable (and wise) to set your own limits about what kinds of activities you wish to engage in and to stick to those limits; to learn to take control of her sexuality; to overcome the fear of sexuality that tends to pervade many people's lives; and to think critically about sex, power, and love, and how she wants to put these explosive and powerful elements together (after all, there are so many rewarding ways to live).

On the other hand, stripping is still stigmatized work, which means that it does involve personal challenges that should not be glossed over—there will always (at least in the current cultural climate) be those individuals who see strippers as "trash." Stripping is also physical labor: it can be grueling at times, dirty (literally, not figuratively), exhausting, and downright boring. But so can waitressing! Doing physical and menial labor is the fate of many teenagers, and such work is accompanied by the benefits of low personal investment, flexibility, a lack of required skills and training, and low competition. Some of us find stripping to be far preferable to taking orders all night and delivering burgers and fries to surly or amorous customers. Stripping, of course, is also premised on a certain kind of youth and attractiveness, and I would hate for her to put too much stake in what her body looks like over what she can accomplish. However, at least on some level, many of the service industries are premised on appearance. Girls are hired at other jobs for their appearance or are successful in them because they have a particular kind of middle-class girly look. In some ways, the explicitness of stripping can be a relief from some of the more covert ways that women are sexualized at work and elsewhere.

Categorizing women as Madonnas or whores, "girls you date" and "girl you sleep with," good girls or sluts, has a long and unfortunate history that will not be overturned without a struggle. And women who strip or work in other realms of the sex industry will likely continue to find themselves fighting against these kinds of labels and the judgments that accompany them. But one hope that I would have for my daughter, and yours, is that she could grow up in a world where some women are not highly valued at the expense of other women and where a woman's sexual desire, interest, experience, pleasure, or mistakes are truly her own.

14

Labor Organizing in the Skin Trade: Tales of a Peep Show Prole

Miss Mary Ann

"Two, four, six, eight, don't come here to masturbate!" sounds a little like something the Moral Majority might have chanted back in the 1980s, but this catchy slogan was actually a battle cry for fair treatment on the job. A few confused bystanders assumed my co-workers and I were antiporn zealots protesting our favorite sleaze merchant. Not exactly—the sex business was our bread and butter. We were strippers picketing for better working conditions at the nude theater that employed us, organizing what would later become the only strippers' union in the country. Our boss had just fired a dancer. The company claimed she was fired for "disrupting other employees," but we knew the real reason was her union activism. The dancer, "Summer," was a single mom with a three-year-old to support. Relations with management had been rocky ever since we started talking union, but Summer's termination sparked an all-out war. It was a Saturday, the union office was closed, and we couldn't get a hold of our union rep. We were on our own. Less than twenty-four hours after Summer was fired, and dozens of phone calls later, close to half the staff of dancers, cashiers, and janitors showed up at work on their day off to protest. With picket signs and leaflets in hand, we poured into the manager's office and demanded Summer's job back. The manager told us to get out. Our picket line went up immediately.

I dance at the Lusty Lady in San Francisco. The place isn't a strip club with a stage and a staff of lapdancers working the audience. It's a peep show—a mirrored box of naked women, writhing and undulating behind glass for masturbating voyeurs. The customers are separated from one another in individual, broom closet-sized booths, and watch the dancers through crotch-level windows. A quarter buys a customer a fifteen-second glimpse of female flesh before the window's shutter closes; most manage to ejaculate before they've spent five bucks. Budget masturbators can complete the task at hand for as little as seventy-five cents by jerking away in the dark, only depositing another quarter when their mental snapshot of us has completely dissipated.

The reporters flocking to cover our organizing drive often had a difficult time understanding what we do as "work," but the job has always been defined in *my* mind by the repetitive manual labor it demands. Punch a time clock, spot an open window, make eye contact, pout, wink, swivel your hips a little, put a stiletto-clad foot up on the windowsill to reveal an eyeful of your two most marketable orifices, fondle your tits, smack your ass, stroke whatever pubic hair you haven't shaven off, repeat these ten steps until the customer comes, then move on to the next window, repeat the process until your shifts are over, punch out.

Some call it the fast food of the sex industry: we produce assembly-line orgasms.

Three of the peep show's thirteen windows were made of one-way glass; the customers could see us, but we couldn't see them. For years, the Lusty Lady attracted amateur pornographers who'd set up shop behind the one-way windows. They videotaped and photographed us with alarming regularity, usually without our knowledge, and always without our consent or compensation. We only discovered how widespread the problem was because absentminded cameramen would occasionally forget to cover the telltale, red "on" light before they started filming. Whenever a dancer looked down and noticed a red light in the window she was dancing for, her impulse was usually to break through the glass and destroy the film. But she'd always resist, fighting the wave of fury and nausea that would inevitably hit her, and call security instead. More often than not though, it would be too late, the guy would get away. Where would that stolen image resurface? Who would see it? How many others were making money off it?

We complained to theater management repeatedly, and asked the company to remove the one-way glass to make it easier for us to spot the video cameras. Management refused and told us to "get another job" if we didn't like it. Despite the company's no camera policy, management insisted that unpaid porn stardom was an occupational hazard we had to accept. We disagreed, and turned to the Exotic Dancers Alliance (EDA), a San Francisco sex worker advocacy group set up by the original plaintiffs in the class-action lawsuit against the Mitchell Brothers' O' Farrell Theater. The EDA put us in touch with local 790 of the Service Employees International Union (SEIU), and convinced the local's initially reluctant organizing staff to take a risk on us, despite disapproval from union higher-ups.

As soon as we announced our plans to unionize, management removed the one-ways, but also refused to recognize the union, and hired a law firm infamous for busting unions. Though the one-ways were gone, other problems at work were still festering: management played favorites, the company's disciplinary policy was unwritten and inconsistently applied, dancers had their pay permanently cut in half for missing a staff meeting or calling in sick, and were suspended for not "having fun" and were fired for even more ambiguous reasons. The female managers who enforced these draconian policies always did so with a smile, insisting we worked at "the best" strip joint in town because we got free hot chocolate and weren't required to suck the boss's dick in exchange for our employment. The company's "sex positive, dancer-friendly" reputation was for the most part a hollow marketing ploy. We had virtually no recourse if we were treated unfairly, and anyone who complained was quickly labeled "disruptive" or "disrespectful." We knew a union contract could temper these injustices and hold the company accountable for its actions.

In the summer of 1996 we decided to go through with a National Labor Relations Board union election. If we won the election, the company would be legally obligated to negotiate a contract with us. Management prepared for the vote by running an antiunion propaganda campaign. Managers held a series of mandatory group meetings, excluded the organizers, and told workers the union would impose exorbitant dues (in reality, about four dollars a week), union officials would "force" us to strike (workers always vote on whether to strike), or fine us for "disagreeing" with them (one of many straight-out lies). The company told us a union would destroy the Lusty Lady "family" (fine with us—in that family, we were the kids and management the parents), and union reps would "bargain away" the rights and benefits we did have during contract negotiations (in reality, other dancers were at the bargaining table negotiating the contract with management, and the workers all vote on the final agreement—the Jimmy Hoffa-style secret, back-room deals between union reps and management the company "warned" us about never materialized). Management put two key organizers on "final warning" for bogus infractions, and spread rumors that they were "harassing" and "intimidating" other dancers. Despite the lies, deceptive leaflets, threats, harassment of union activists, and scripted, tear-filled pleas to give the company a "second chance," we stuck it out and won the election fifty-seven to fifteen. We named our SEIU chapter the Exotic Dancers Union.

We spent the months following the election attempting to negotiate a contract with the company. But instead of working out an agreement with us, company lawyers spent most of the bargaining sessions engaged in performance art that easily rivaled our own in caliber and affectation. Like a stripper who waits until the end of the song to wiggle out of her panties, the lawyers kept their client paying by teasing us with lengthy diatribes, each bargaining session's invective more scathing than the last, the union's planned demise just around the corner. They were paid by the hour, and their time-wasting strategies were impressive. For example, they spent days insisting that dancers were "sexually harassing" each other by using the "scurrilous, offensive, and derogatory term 'pussy'" in the workplace. (Despite the word's "scurrilous" qualities, one lawyer in particular delighted in repeating this term as often as possible.) Nevermind that our workplace is a smut palace, the lawyers repeatedly ignored our efforts to discuss things like sick pay and grievance rights, and flooded us with contract proposals outlawing foul-mouthed hussies instead.

Although the lawyers turned out to be far better whores than we could ever aspire to be, attorney-customer comparisons were also inevitable and hard to avoid. At the end of one particularly tedious bargaining session, the star of the company's legal team even copped to the similarity. "An attorney is but a condom," he bragged, "protecting the prick who's screwing someone else." That line was the first and last piece of honesty we got from this guy. After getting paid to watch middle-aged men in power suits masturbate to us every day at work, our tolerance for all the rhetorical circle jerking we had to endure for free at the bargaining table quickly began to wane. As the lawyers' bargaining session rants wore on, we'd begin to imagine them with their ties flung over their shoulders, the way we were accustomed to seeing their peers in the peep booths at work. (This fashion trend guards against the embarrassing possibility of returning to the office with a semen-splattered tie.)

We resolved the "pussy" issue, but then company lawyers began insisting management needed the right to fire any dancer who'd been with the company for more than a year and a half. Since customers need "variety," they reasoned, termination of long-term dancers was a "legitimate business need." In this industry, seniority is a liability; strip joints *want* a high turnover. This was a temporary job, a short-term assignment, the duration of which was determined by a byzantine and arcane set of constantly changing criteria that managers would use to justify firing dancers who got too "old" or too uppity. One dancer's "sultry stare" was another's "scornful glare." One month our run-of-the-mill pelvic grinding would be "interactive" and "fun," the managers would tell us, but the next month they'd call it "repetitive" and "boring." Countless trees died needlessly to sustain the Lusty Lady's almost fetishistic obsession with documenting our "job performance" in an extensive collection of personnel files they maintained on us. It was a damn *peep show* for chrissakes, not a psychotropic drug study, or a Broadway production for that matter! Management knew we'd never agree to contract language that would codify the company's "right" to fire us at will—"legitimate business need" or not—but they were trying to wear us down, and make us give up.

We didn't give up, and a few months into this routine, we staged a job action to protest the slow pace at the bargaining table. The Lusty Lady is the only place in town any eighteen-year-old kid (or forty-year-old executive) can watch live, gyrating, three-dimensional, *Hustler*-style beaver shots, inches from his face, for half the price of a donut. (No, we don't hustle "peeps" for quarters; we're paid by the hour to perform for whoever's watching.) The two-bit pussy show is the Lusty Lady's signature commodity, and on "No Pink" day the goods weren't for sale. We continued to dance nude, but kept our legs demurely closed. The marquee outside still said XXX, but the show we put on was probably somewhere between PG-13 and R. Almost every dancer who worked that day took part in the action, and frantic managers responded to our newfound modesty by firing Summer.

The attempt to intimidate and divide us backfired. We retaliated by picketing the theater for the next two days and management fired back with a lockout. They closed the show, and the dancers scheduled to work lost two days' pay, but we stuck together and kept the picket line going. Most customers steered clear of the commotion, some were supportive, a few mistook us for antiporn Christians, but only a handful braved a tongue-lashing from the crowd and crossed our picket line. Apparently deluded by their legal counsel into thinking the union was "all talk," managers were stunned that we actually had the balls (and the solidarity) to walk the walk. After a two-day stalemate, the company caved in, rehired Summer, and finally began to cooperate at the bargaining table. Management quit talking about the "need" to fire long-term dancers, and offered us a raise instead.

Ultimately, management didn't agree to all of our demands, and there was talk of a strike, but we eventually ratified a first contract in April 1997, and we've renewed the agreement each year since. There's still a sizable gap between profits for the company and wages for the workers, but we won rights, job security, sick pay, automatic raises, and a guarantee the one-way windows won't return from a company that probably never intended on reaching a contract at all, in an industry infamous for regarding its workforce as disposable.

Although the Lusty Lady is currently the only unionized nude theater in the country, our success sparked similar organizing campaigns at other clubs and theaters in Alaska, Pennsylvania, and California. Dressing rooms across the nation are full of disgruntled strippers who want to do more than gripe about their plight.

To learn how to pull off a do-it-yourself union-organizing campaign at your own neighborhood girlie show, call the Exotic Dancers Union at 510-465-0122 X461 or visit www.LiveNudeGirlsUnite.com.

Bibliography

Allen, R. 1991. *Horrible Prettiness: Burlesques and American Culture*. Chapel Hill, NC: University of North Carolina Press.

Allison, A. 1993. "Dominating Men: Male Dominance on Company Expense in a Japanese Hostess Club." *Genders* 16: 1–16.

Althusser, L. 2001. "Ideology and Ideological State Apparatuses." *Lenin and Philosophy and Other Essays*. Ben Brewster, trans. New York City: Monthly Review. 85–126.

Atkinson, T. G. 1974. *Amazon Odyssey*. New York City: Links.

Bartky, S. L. 1991. *Femininity and Domination: Studies in the Phenomenology of Oppression*. New York City: Routledge.

Baumgardner, J. and A. Richards. 2000. *Manifesta: Young Women, Feminism, and the Future*. New York City: Farrar, Straus, and Giroux.

Bell, H., L. Sloan, and C. Strickling. 1998. "Exploiter or Exploited: Topless Dancers Reflect on Their Experiences." *Affilia* 13.3: 352–68.

Bildstein, J. 1996. *The King of Clubs*. New York: Barricade Books.

Bishop, R. and Robinson, L. 1998. *Night Market: Sexual Cultures and the Thai Economic Miracle*. New York: Routledge.

Blanchard, B. 1999. "Tales of a Tokyo Stripper." *Salon.com* (May 28) http: / / www.salon.com / travel / wlust / 1999 / 05 / 28 / stripper.

Bordo, S. 1999. *The Male Body: A New Look at Men in Public and in Private*. New York City, Farrar, Straus, and Giroux.

Brooks, G. R. 1995. *The Centerfold Syndrome: How Men Can Overcome Objectification and Achieve Intimacy with Women.* San Francisco, CA: Jossey-Bass Publishers.

Burana, L. 2001. *Strip City: A Stripper's Farewell Journey Across America.* New York City: Miramax Books.

Califia, P., ed. 1994. *Doing It for Daddy.* Los Angeles, CA: Alyson.

Chancer, L. S. 1998. *Reconcilable Differences: Confronting Beauty, Pornography, and the Future of Feminism.* Berkeley, CA: University of California Press.

Chapkis, W. 1997. *Live Sex Acts: Women Performing Erotic Labor.* New York City: Routledge.

Dubisch, J. 1995. "Lovers in the Field: Sex, Dominance, and the Female Anthropologist." *Taboo: Sex, Identity, and Erotic Subjectivity in Anthropological Fieldwork.* D. Kulick and M. Wilson, eds. New York City: Routledge Press. 28–50.

Egan, R. D. 2003. "I'll be Your Fantasy Girl, If You'll be My Money Man: Mapping Desire, Fantasy, and Power in Two Exotic Dance Clubs." *Journal of Psychoanalysis, Culture, and Society* (8) 1:109–120.

Frank, K. 2002. *G-Strings and Sympathy: Strip Club Regulars and Male Desire.* Durham, NC: Duke University Press.

———. 1998. "The Production of Identity and the Negotiation of Intimacy in a Gentleman's Club." *Sexualities* 2: 175–201.

Gottlieb, D. 2003. *Final Girl.* New York City: Soft Skull.

Grasse, N. 1999. "Dancing Lessons." *Salon.com* (July 23) http://www.salon.com/books/it/1999/07/23/stripping.

Hanna, J. L. 1998. "Undressing the First Amendment and Corsetting the Striptease Dancer." *Drama Review.* 42: 38–69.

Heywood, L. and J. Drake. 1997. *Third Wave Agenda: Being Feminist, Doing Feminism.* Minneapolis, MN: University of Minnesota Press.

Jarrett, L. 1997. *Stripping in Time.* London, England: Pandora Press.

Katz, J. 1996. *The Invention of Heterosexuality.* New York City: Plume.

Lasch, C. 1979. *The Culture of Narcissism: American Life in an Age of Diminishing Expectations.* New York City: W. W. Norton and Company.

Liepe-Levinson, K. 2002. *Strip Show: Performances of Gender and Desire.* New York City: Routledge.

Merleau-Ponty, M. 1968. *The Visible and the Invisible.* Evanston, IL: Northwestern University Press.

Morgan, Peggy. 1987. "Living on the Edge." *Sex Work: Writings by Women in the Sex Industry.* Frederique Delacoste and Priscilla Alexander, eds. San Francisco, CA: Cleis.

Oliker, S. J. 1989. *Best Friends and Marriage: Exchange Among Women.* Berkeley, CA: University of California, 1989.

Pride, Ray. 1998. "Peter Berg Does Very Bad Things and a Whole Lot More." *IndieWire* (November 30). http://www.indiewire.com/people/int_Berg_Peter_981130.html.

Projansky, S. 2001. *Watching Rape: Film and Television in Postfeminist Culture.* New York City: New York University Press.

Queen, C. 1997. *Real Live Nude Girl.* Pittsburgh, PA: Cleis Press Inc.

Ronai-Rambo, C. 1998. "Sketching with Derrida: An Ethnography of Researcher/Erotic Dancer." *Qualitative Inquiry.* 4: 405–20.

———. 1992. "The Reflexive Self Through Narrative: A Night in the Life of an Erotic Dancer/Researcher." *Investigating Subjectivity: Research on Lived Experience.* Carolyn Ellis and Michael G. Flaherty, eds. Thousand Oaks, CA: Sage Press. 102–124.

Rubin, G. 1992. "Thinking Sex: Notes for a Radical Theory of the Politics of Sexuality." *Pleasure and Danger: Exploring Female Sexuality.* Carole S. Vance, ed. London, England: Pandora. 267–319.

Russo, V. 1981. *The Celluloid Closet: Homosexuality in the Movies.* New York City: Harper and Row.

Smith, D. 2003. "Phenomenology," *The Stanford Encyclopedia of Philosophy.* Edward N. Zalta, ed. http://plato.stanford.edu/ archives/win2003/entries/phenomenology.

Steinberg, J. 1998. "Some Room of Their Own: Dancers Win Claim Against Mitchell Brothers; Organize in Anchorage." *Comes Naturally* #73.

Stock, Wendy. "Sex as Commodity: Men and the Sex Industry." *Men and Sex: New Psychological Perspectives.* Ronald F. Levant and Gary R. Brooks, eds. New York City: John Wiley & Sons, Inc. 100–32.

Tanenbaum, L. 2000. *Slut! Growing Up Female With A Bad Reputation.* New York City: Seven Stories Press.

Tiefer, L. 1995. *Sex Is Not A Natural Act and Other Essays*. Boulder, CO: Westview Press.

Warner, M. 1999. *The Trouble with Normal: Sex, Politics, and the Ethics of Queer Life.* New York City: Free Press.

Willis, S. 2000. " 'Style,' Posture, and Idiom: Tarantino's Figures of Masculinity." *Reinventing Film Studies*. Christine Gledhill and Linda Williams, eds. London, England: Oxford University Press. 279–95.

Williams, L. 1999. *Hard Core: Power, Pleasure, and the Frenzy of the Visible*. Berkley, CA: University of California Press.

Wolf, Naomi. 1999. *Promiscuities: The Secret Struggle for Womanhood.* New York City: Random House.

Contributor Bios

Jamie Berger moved from New York to San Francisco in 1992 after finishing a master's degree in poetry. He hasn't written a poem since, but that could change any day now. His two monologues "Knowing the Questions" and "Regrets Only" had extended runs in San Francisco and New York. His writing has appeared in the *San Francisco Chronicle, McSweeneys.net,* the *Sun, Negative Capability, Columbia* Magazine, *Planet* Magazine, *In Posse Review, Watchword,* and elsewhere. Peep shows, strip clubs, and the like have been pleasing and tormenting him since 1982. See also: www.jamiebergerwords.com.

Susan Bremer has retired from exotic dancing and has founded Self Appeal® and produced the "Art of Sensual Dance® for Every Body" for DVD and VHS. She resides in Oakland California where she lectures and gives workshops on sensuality, striptease, and body acceptance and empowerment. For more information about Susan and her work go to www.selfappeal.com.

Emile Blauche is the nom-de-plume of a strip-club denizen whose essays have appeared in academic and nonacademic journals. He enjoys the company of dancers more than that of any other professional on earth. He once found a dancer who was actually impressed by his Ph.D., and so it should be, that is there was only one, that is . . .

R. Danielle Egan (Ph.D. Boston College 2000) is an Assistant Professor of Sociology at St. Lawrence University in Canton, New York. She has published work in *Critical Sociology, Body and Society, Deviant Behavior, Sexualities,* and *The Journal of Psychoanalysis, Society and Culture*. In addition to her work on exotic dance, she has written on post 9/11 rhetoric, pedagogy, and popular culture. Her current research is on childhood sexuality.

Alison Fensterstock is a freelance writer and occasional burlesque and go-go dancer living in New Orleans. She is a founding producer of the annual burlesque convention Tease-O-Rama.

Katherine Frank is a cultural anthropologist (Ph.D. Duke University, 1999), fiction writer, and former exotic dancer. Her first book, *G-Strings and Sympathy: Strip Club Regulars and Male Desire* (2002) is an exploration of the motivations and experiences of the heterosexual male customers of strip clubs. She has also written on eating disorders, gender, pornography, feminism, and monogamy. Her fiction has appeared in *The Sonora Review, The Crescent Review, Black Sheets, Vixen,* and *Gauntlet,* among other publications. She is currently affiliated with the sociology department at the University of Wisconsin-Madison, studying the ways that contemporary American couples negotiate sexual exclusivity in marriage and working on an ethnography of swinging. For more information, visit her Web site: www.katefrank.com.

Merri Lisa Johnson is an English professor (Ph.D. Binghamton University, 2000), creative nonfiction writer, and former exotic dancer. Her edited collection, *Jane Sexes It Up: True Confessions of Feminist Desire* (Four Walls Eight Windows, 2000), formulates a third wave feminist sexual politics; contributors combine feminist theory with creative nonfiction to negotiate the space between their feminist ideals and the messiness of lived sexuality (in romance, marriage, sex work, and fetish play). She has published essays on third wave feminism and adultery, feminist television studies, stripping, and the uses of autobiography as a form of social criticism. Her article on representations of marriage on

HBO's *Six Feet Under* is forthcoming in *Discourse*. Johnson teaches American literature and women's studies at Coastal Carolina University.

Shelly Manaster was a Ph. D candidate in the Department of Anthropology at the Graduate Faculty of Political and Social Science in NYC. Her dissertation focused on women in the sex industry who earned their living giving lap dances in San Francisco. She worked in numerous clubs in San Francisco over a five-year period. She was also a writer of short stories, a mean pool player and overly indulgent with her Italian greyhound, Wallaby. She passed away on January 1st, 2001, after being in a serious car accident while in Greece.

Miss Mary Ann has retired from the sex industry, but continues to work with dancers who want help starting their own union-organizing campaigns. She lives in San Francisco with her young son.

John Smith is a pseudonym for a psychology professor at a liberal arts college in the Midwest. He teaches human sexuality courses and would like to believe his visits to the strip clubs qualify for a tax deduction. He became a regular after a visit to a club in August 2001.

Jo Weldon first stripped onstage in 1978, a tad underage at the *Rocky Horror Picture Show*, flinging her boa about with a passion that persists to this day. She mounted the stage professionally as soon as she was of age, and over time she advanced to the level of feature dancer, booked to headline at strip joints across the continent, always keeping the ladies of burlesque in mind as she created her elaborately costumed and themed acts. She has been studying the art and craft of striptease for over two decades. In the 1990s she accompanied some of New York's most innovative and talented performance artists into the national neoburlesque scene, where her prior experience proved invaluable in developing the outrageous, sexy, versatile persona of Jo Boobs. She also teaches burlesque and lapdancing workshops. For more information, visit her Web site: http://www.gstringsforever.com.

Endnotes

1. Heywood and Drake, 1997.
2. Califa, P., 1994, 11.
3. Chapkis, 1997, 29.
4. Chancer, 1998, 270.
5. For more on the history of burlesque, see Allen, 1991; on the development of striptease, see Jarrett, 1997; on emotional labor in strip clubs, see Ronai-Rambo, 1998, 1992; Egan, 2003; Frank, 2002, 1998.
6. Bell, Sloan, and Strickling, 1998.
7. Liepe-Levinson, 2002.
8. Frank, 2002.
9. Williams, 1999. See also Liepe-Levinson, 2002.
10. Hanna, 1998.
11. Liepe-Levinson, 2002.
12. MSNBC, February 17, 2005.
13. Steinberg, 1998.
14. Ira Levin quoted in Chapkis, 1997, 31.
15. For more on this see Tanenbaum, 2000.
16. Katz, 1996.
17. I would like to thank Mary Haught, Rita Hewlett, Allen Shelton, and Steve Papson for commenting on the "readability" of this article. I would also like to thank Kate Frank and Lisa Johnson for making me "push further" with this piece. You two rock!

18. Smith, 2003.
19. Dubisch, 1995.
20. All individuals and places in this piece have been given pseudonyms to protect their anonymity.
21. Merleau-Ponty, 1968.
22. It is important to note that Merleau-Ponty assumes consent in his philosophical premise.
23. Chapkis, 1997.
24. Kayla was my stage name.
25. Merleau-Ponty, 1968.
26. Burana, 2001.
27. This piece is dedicated to Christine Warner. Her sense of humor, sharp wit, great conversations on long car rides home, and brilliant lessons on how to wear six-inch Lucite heels made my time dancing far more interesting.
28. The research discussed in this article was assisted by a fellowship from the Sexuality Research Fellowship Program of the Social Science Research Council with funds provided by the Ford Foundation.
29. Bildstein, 1996, 22.
30. Lasch, 1977.
31. Allison, 1995; Bishop and Robinson, 1998; Chapkis, 1997.
32. Oliker, 1989, 57.
33. Tiefer, 1995.
34. Bordo, 1999.
35. Tiefer, 142.
36. Brooks, 1995; Stock, 1997.
37. Queen, 1997, 130.
38. Bartky, 1991.
39. Originally published in *The Sun* as "Peep Show."
40. I attribute this point to Gayle Rubin, who writes that antiporn rhetoric in feminism "implies that sexism originates within the commercial sex industry and subsequently infects the rest of society," a position she rejects as "sociologically nonsense." "The sex industry is hardly a feminist utopia," she concedes: "It reflects

the sexism that exists in the society as a whole. We nee
lyze and oppose the manifestations of gender inequality spe
to the sex industry. But this is not the same as attempting to wip
out commercial sex" (301–02).

41. Chapkis, 1997, 71.
42. Chapkis 1997, 79–80.
43. My vision of "liberated" sexualities arose from a sheltered, provincial culture, in which "France" looks from afar like one big strip club and "Mars" is, basically, a gay bar, or so a certain ditty from my childhood told it:

    There's a place in France
    Where the naked ladies dance.
    There's a hole in the wall
    Where the men watch it all.

    There's a place on Mars
    Where the ladies smoke cigars
    And the men don't care
    If they eat their underwear.

    I longed to find this place where it's okay to be naked, to be watched, to smoke cigars, to eat underwear. Strip clubs offered me that place. They became the London, the France, and the visible underpants of my fantasies.
44. Morgan, 1987, 25.
45. Califia writes, "As horrible as child abuse is, even more children are damaged by their parents' ignorance or panic about sex. Most parents still punish or shame their children for masturbating or asking questions about their own anatomy or human reproduction" (11).
46. Warner, 1999, 38.
47. Warner, 1999, 89.
48. Bartky, 1991, 74.
49. In a documentary on media representations of gays and lesbians,

The Celluloid Closet, screenwriter Arthur Laurents reflects on this broad category of sex bashing in the history of American film, noting the persistent plot link between sexual experimentation and violence or death: "I think the fate of gay characters in American literature, plays, [and] films is really the fate of all characters who are sexually free. You may pay. You must suffer."

50. From *The Sopranos* discussion board: http://www.the-sopranos.com/db/ep32_review.htm.
51. Sarah Projansky describes this "paradox of discursively *increasing* . . . the very thing a text is working against" in films about rape. *The Accused*, for instance, "emphasizes the horror of rape and illustrates the idea that even if a woman dresses and dances provocatively in a public bar, she is not responsible if a gang rape follows. But, the graphic representation is also explicit in its visual and aural depiction of sexual violence toward women, thus increasing the amount of violence against women that exists in popular-culture representations" (96).
52. Willis, 2000, 281.
53. Althusser, 104.
54. The ageism inherent in this designation of stage-appropriate girls and audience-appropriate girls marks yet another constraint on the expression of female sexuality.
55. This essay is dedicated to the official girl squad of Coastal Carolina University's English Department—Maria Bachman, Maggie Ivanova, and Shannon Stewart—because one day I said, "Let's go to a strip club" and they said, "okay."
56. http://msnbc.msn.com/id/4741047/; http://www.zap2it.com/movies/news/story/0,1259,—16232,00.html.
57. http://people.aol.com/people/articles/0,19736,1017005,00.html.

List of Copyrights